EAST OF
LO MONTHANG
IN THE LAND OF M·U·S·T·A·N·G

*Tange village, river and chortens; snowcapped mountains of Dolpo beyond
the west bank of the Kali Gandaki.*

EAST OF
LO MONTHANG
IN THE LAND OF M·U·S·T·A·N·G

PETER MATTHIESSEN
PHOTOGRAPHY BY THOMAS LAIRD

SHAMBHALA
Boston
1996

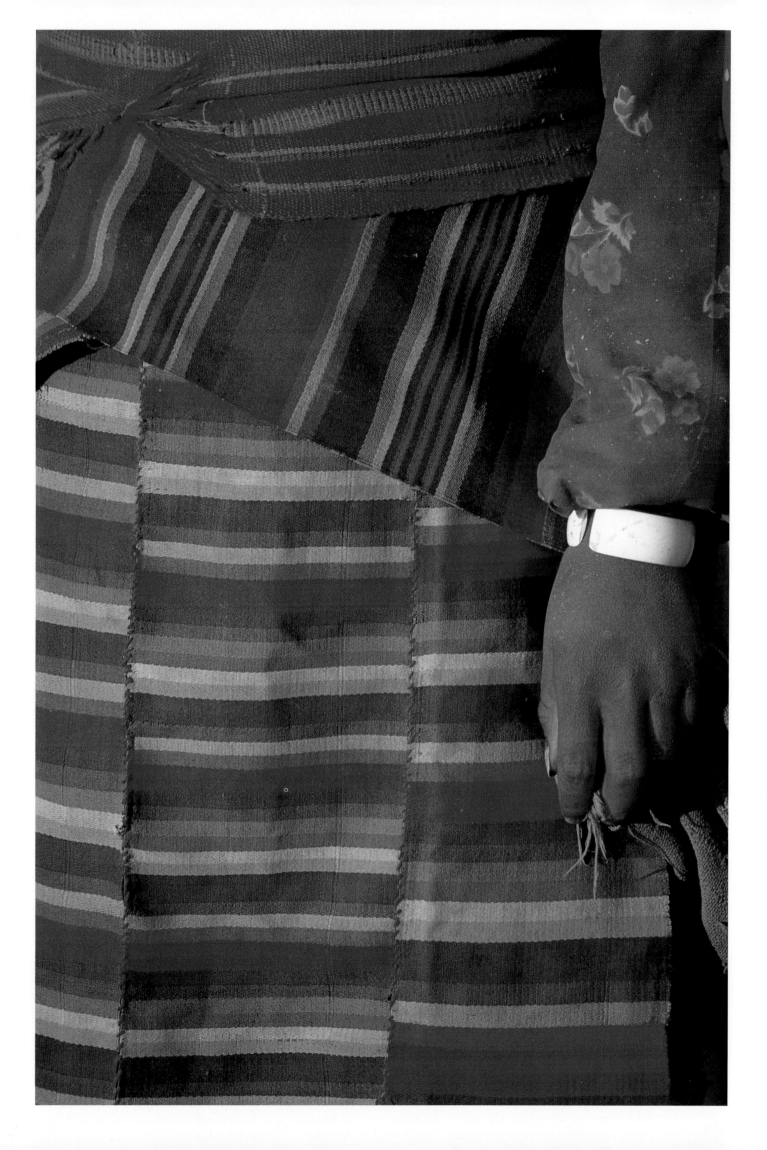

Irrigation water flows from Dhungmara Himal, past the walls of Lo Monthang and out to these fields in front of the capital. The ruins of Kechar Fort at crest of the hill in the middle right, and the Tibetan border runs along the far right horizon.

EAST OF LO MONTHANG: IN THE LAND OF MUSTANG

Shambhala Publications, Inc.
Horticultural Hall
300 Massachusetts Avenue
Boston, Massachusetts 02115

TEXT © 1995 PETER MATTHIESSEN
PHOTOS & CAPTIONS © 1995 THOMAS LAIRD

9 8 7 6 5 4 3 2 1

First Paperback Edition
Printed in Hong Kong

Distributed in the United States by Random House, Inc.,
and in Canada by Random House of Canada Ltd.

The Library of Congress catalogues the hardcover edition of this book as follows:

Matthiessen, Peter
   East of Lo Monthang: in the Land of Mustang /
   Peter Matthiessen; photography by Thomas Laird.—1st Shambhala ed.
      p.   cm.
      ISBN 1-57062-131-4
      ISBN 1-57062-226-4 (paperback)
      1. Mustang (Nepal)—Description and travel.   2. Matthiessen,
Peter—Journeys—Nepal—Mustang.   3. Laird, Thomas—Journeys—
Nepal—Mustang I. Laird, Thomas.   II. Title.
DS495.8.M87M37   1995   95-204
915.496—dc20   CIP

Edited by Elizabeth Rhudy
Copyedited by Mary Orr
Designed by David Hurst

PAGE 1 ~ *trail-side chorten near Charang with the Annapurna Himal beyond*

PAGE 4 ~ *Lama Tashi Tenzing's prayer beads, key chain, and ritual dagger*

PAGE 5 ~ *hand-spun, hand-woven wool apron of nomad woman*

PAGES 8~9 ~ *Raja Jigme Parwar Bista, returning from Tibet, sets out across the 16,000-foot border plateau — Birkuti and Damodar Himal behind.*

PAGE 10 ~ *Trangmar, or "Red Cliff Village" with Annapurna and Nilgiri Himal*

PAGE 11 ~ *Raja Jigme at the end of Tiji Ceremony*

CONTENTS

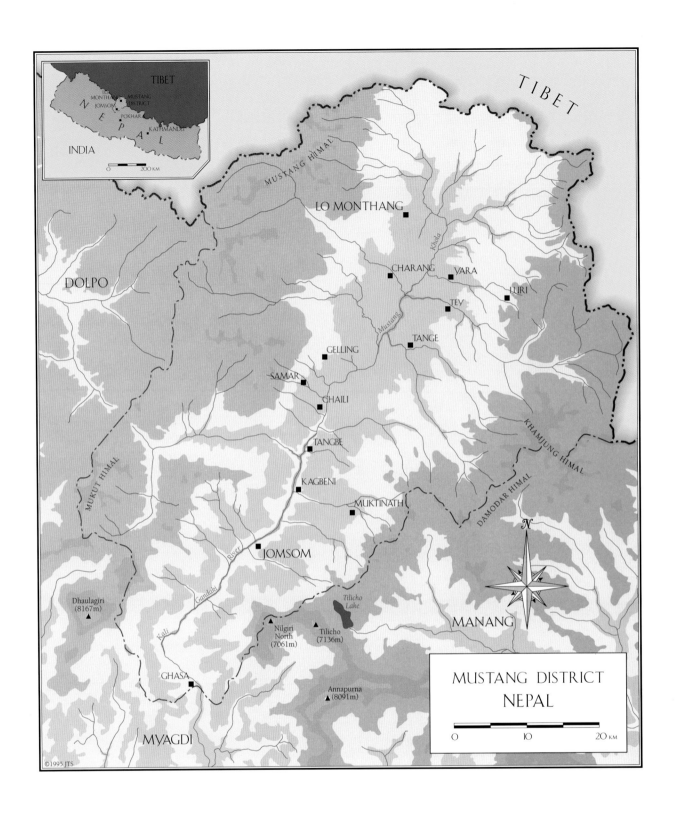

TIBET

INDIA

NEPAL

TIBET

DOLPO

LO MONTHANG

CHARANG
VARA
LURI
TEV
TANGE

GELLING

SAMAR
CHAILI

TANGBE

KAGBENI

MUKTINATH

JOMSOM

Dhaulagiri
(8167m)

Nilgiri
North
(7061m)

Tilicho
(7136m)

Tilicho
Lake

MANANG

GHASA

Annapurna
(8091m)

MUKUT HIMAL

MUSTANG HIMAL

KHAMJUNG HIMAL

DAMODAR HIMAL

Khola

Mustang

Gandaki
River

Kali

N

MYAGDI

© 1995 JTS

MUSTANG DISTRICT
NEPAL

0   10   20 KM

WINGS OF DAYBREAK

TWENTY YEARS AGO, WHEN I FIRST CAME TO POKHARA, IN central Nepal, there were no roads farther north or west; we travelled on foot for two hundred and fifty miles west across the Kali Gandaki River and north again across the Himalaya to the old Tibetan kingdom known as Dolpo. Today, a motor road as far as the Kali Gandaki has been completed, and there is an airstrip at Jomsom, at the northern end of the Kali Gandaki gorge. From Jomson we shall proceed north on horseback into Lo, an ancient and long-isolated land surrounded on three sides by Tibet.

On the wings of daybreak on this bright day of mid-May, 1992, the twin-engine Otter flying northwest from Pokhara crosses the stepped greens of the rice terraces in the central hills and is still climbing as it makes a long curve north toward the great portal between the shining peaks of Annapurna and Dhaulagiri. The massifs rise more than 26,500 feet (or five miles high), and the river beneath, rushing south through the Himalaya from the raja of Lo on the Tibetan border to the Ganges plain, lies in the deepest gorge on earth. The airplane is so far below the peaks and so close to the flank of Annapurna that one sees pink blossoms on huge rhododendrons on the lower slopes. But already this forest is giving way to stands of pine and fir, and very soon the conifers thin out, then subside entirely on brown mountainsides and sandy mesas. These are the high treeless deserts in the Himalayan rain shadow, which extend northward to the Tibetan Plateau and on to the Kunlun Mountains of the Central Asian desert — the dry wastes of what geographers once called "the dead heart of Asia."

flying between Dhaulagiri and Annapurna

Under the Dhaulagiri icefall just north of the gorge, the riverbed abruptly widens, as houses appear in flat-roofed clusters quite unlike the thatched dwellings in the south. With no room to circle, the plane, scarcely descending, flies straight out of the mountains onto the Jomsom strip, exchanges passengers and cargo, and flies out again, straight down the canyon. This is the first and last plane of the day, fleeing Jomsom before the blasting wind rises in the mid-morning heat of the Indian plain and is sucked northward through this awesome breach by the low pressure of the mountain deserts, to whip and scour the ridges and plateaus.

Jomsom, at 8,800 feet, lies at twice the altitude of Pokhara, though scarcely a third of the altitude of Nilgiri, the snow peak at the northwest corner of the Annapurna cirque that towers behind the town like an ice wall. Upriver, beyond blue shadows of the northern mountains, lies the land of Lo.

Outside the Buddhist Himalaya and the high deserts to the north, Lo is better known as "Mustang," a British corruption of the name of its fort-city, Lo Monthang. In its great days, between A.D. 1400 and 1600, when it dominated the Kali Gandaki trade between India and Tibet, Lo was a borderland of Ngari or West Tibet, a vast realm extending from Lo and Dolpo in the east to Ladakh in the west. (According to Sven Hedin, the Swedish explorer, it was known in Tibet as "The Land of the King of the South.") In the 17th century, a declining Lo was forced to pay levies on its river trade to the Kingdom of Jumla, farther west, and after 1795, when Jumla was defeated by the rising power of the Gorkha warriors who were carving out the Kingdom of Nepal, Lo transferred its levies (one hundred pieces of silver and a horse, it has been said) to the new kingdom. Though akin to Tibetan culture as well as language, Lo supported Nepal in the war with Tibet sixty years later, thus affirming its right to its ancient feudal system of Rajas and serfs. The title 'Raja of Mustang' is still given by His Majesty The King of Nepal, to the Raja of Lo, even today. Though serfdom was formally abolished in 1956 the villages still supply some unpaid labor for the raja's fields and other community duties.

Reports in the West that such a place existed date back to 1793, when an English traveller named W. J. Kirkpatrick was told of Lo Monthang as "a place of some note in upper Tibet or Bhot," but very few travellers reached Nepal before 1950, and fewer still were permitted to go anywhere beyond Kathmandu. Since Tibet was also "a forbidden land," Lo remained virtually unknown. Excepting a man named Hari Ram, of the Survey of India, who reached Lo Monthang in 1873, the first foreigner ever to set foot in Mustang was a Swiss

A plane circles Jomsom, passing in front of Nilgiri Himal.

OPPOSITE ~ *The village of Kagbeni with Thorung Pass beyond.*

16

geologist, Toni Hagen, who explored the Himalayan regions in 1950. "To the best of my knowledge, I was the first European ever to lay eyes on the raja's capital city, in which his mud-walled and glass-windowed four-story palace was the outstanding architectural glory" (Toni Hagen, "Afoot in Roadless Nepal," *National Geographic*, March, 1960). Next to arrive at Lo Monthang was the Tibetan scholar Giuseppe Tucci, who made a quick visit in 1952 (*Journey to Mustang,* Kathmandu, Ratna Pustak Bhandar, 1977); he was followed by a young

Frenchman, Michel Peissel, (*Mustang, the Forbidden Kingdom,* New York, E.P. Dutton, 1967) in 1964. Since then, Nepal has discouraged travel into Lo, a protrusion on the five-hundred-mile north border that has been described as "a thumb in the eye of Tibet," especially after 1960, when the kingdom became the base of operations for Khampa guerrillas from east Tibet who were fighting the brutal Chinese occupation of their country. That year, Lo was entirely closed to outside visitors until late 1991, when a new government took over and an American correspondent-photographer named Thomas Laird, one of the few reporters on hand in Kathmandu to cover the 1990 revolution, was awarded a permit for travel in the kingdom. In 1992, a few more permits were issued, and one was obtained for me by Laird, who had been living in Kathmandu for almost twenty years, spoke good Nepali, and was a student of the Tibetan Buddhist culture which, in his opinion, found extraordinary artistic expression in the unfrequented monasteries and palace-forts of the Kali Gandaki River trade route. One day in March 1992, on a spirited impulse that recommended him right from the outset, Laird rang the United States from Kathmandu and invited me, a man he had never met, to go with him into Lo. To judge from his fervent account of Lo, and his own credentials, it seemed that a more qualified travelling companion could scarcely be found. I accepted at once in the same out-of-the-blue spirit.

The village priest of Kagbeni makes offerings to a pre-Buddhist protector deity.

◈ Ghost-Eaters and Border Towns

The inhabitants of Jomsom are mostly traders of the Thakali tribe attracted to this great portal on the Himalayan passage, where the trade based on northern salt (for southern rice) probably dates back at least two thousand years. Here are found the last airstrip, inns, shops, and electricity on the way to Lo. We took a last tea in the inn known as "Om's Home in Jomsom" before walking three hours north up the mighty canyon, leaving the Hindu world of the subcontinent behind.

In these last weeks before the monsoon season when the high glaciers on the Dolpo border to the west release their water, the Kali Gandaki is no more than a swift gray stream snaking back and forth through the shining silver cobbles of a great river bed a quarter mile across. To the west, steep barren cliffs rise toward black peaks of the Dolpo border — Tsartse and Tashi Kang, both close to 20,000 feet — but on the east bank, which climbs more gradually toward the peaks, wild roses — ivory, with yellow stamens — are in flower, and pied wagtails and the beautiful black redstarts come and go. Below the upper gorge, which we shall reach tomorrow, the small villages along the trading route — all but the new outcropping we have just left, called "Airport Jomsom" — lie on the east side of the river.

Off to the west, up a ravine, lies the trail to Tscharka, in Dolpo, and from the east descends the track from Muktinath, an ancient site of old Buddhist and Hindu shrines that is mentioned in the Hindu Vedas. At the teahouse at Eklai Bhattai ("One Lonely Inn"), a sign reads "All Kinds Of Tibetan Somethins Sold Here," and the head of a Tibetan antelope and the stuffed carcass of a *peh-mousa* or Himalayan marmot grace the wall. Here we overtake two river traders carrying towering loads of new bamboo baskets from the south.

Ahead, on terraces that climb up from the river, green fields are flowing in the wind and a walled village and large red gompa or monastery, stand on the cliff edge of a narrows at the bend. The golden greens of the new barley and the blood-red gompa are startling colors in this vast brooding landscape of shale browns and stony grays of cliff and mesa, and dark jagged peaks. Behind the gompa, the turreted palace and old town of sturdy whitewashed houses behind walls is constructed as a fortress, in an age-old defense against wind and brigands. This is Kag or Kagbeni, one of the palace-forts along the trading route subdued when the Kingdom of Lo was formed in the 15th century.

FOLLOWING PAGES ~ *Kagbeni at the end of monsoon, surrounded by pink fields of ripening buckwheat*

As in so many desert mountain villages, all the way west to Afghanistan, Kagbeni's barley fields (a second crop of buckwheat will come later) are irrigated by small aqueducts like manmade brooks, led down along the hillsides from the icy streams that descend from the snow peaks and the glaciers, then braided outward in small aqueducts to the terraced fields along the river cliffs. In places, the whole stream may be used, so that not a drop of the scarce and precious water reaches the river.

Already the wind out of the south is battering the canyon, and hill pigeons are hurtled back and forth over the town. Today is the first full moon of May, celebrated in Lo as the day of birth, enlightenment, and death of the Lord Buddha; the red gompa, together with all the chortens (Buddhist stupas or reliquaries), from small cairn-like monuments with a lone prayer flag on a mountain pass to large entrance chortens at town portals that may include an interior passage and old frescoes, have been freshly daubed with black and ocher clays for the occasion.

Nilgiri Himal glows at sunset as villagers carry Buddhist scriptures around Kagbeni for the May full-moon festival.

OPPOSITE ~ *Bishnaduki of Lo Monthang leads his horse up the Kali Gandaki canyon between Chaili and Tange villages.*

Buddhism in these remote hills has absorbed much of the local witchcraft as well as vestiges of the old pre-Buddhist B'on religion, including the hanging demon-traps — sun crosses, dead hares, and the like — over the doorway and protective shrines — mostly old skulls and horns — upon the roof. Near the gate, a group of men has gathered to renew the grotesque female figure of Kheni, the "Ghost-eater." A large sprawled monster built up in crude-packed clay against a wall, Kheni has red eyes and teeth, breasts pointed up by fiery orange nipples, and even a pubic patch fashioned of goat hair. The patch is claimed, not without pride, by one of her curators, who cries out to us, "Well, then? You need some of this?"

When all is ready, two large Buddha figures and the sacred scriptures, bound in silk cloth and wood boards, are brought forth from the gompa by cropped-head monks in maroon and saffron and borne past the old fort-palace of the town, as the folk rush to touch their foreheads to the books and statues. To lugubrious blartings of twelve-foot horns, short double-reeded horns, hand drums and cymbals, the procession pays homage to the ghost-eaters, not only Kheni but her male equivalent inside the walls (an even larger and more grotesque figure with an erect penis), as demons are banished and all is purified by an incense of burnt juniper. In cosmic renewal, the lama in an orange hood flicks water from old peacock feathers dipped in a silver jug, and a young monk hurls barley seed in all directions. As a kind of spring fertility rite in a hard land, the ceremony needs all the good will from earth deities it can solicit.

Eventually the procession leaves the village. In a cold wind, as the wild pigeons snap and plummet and a bright twilight falls down from the mountains, the folk of Kag make a circumambulation of the fields to ward off demons in the form of malevolent insects.

◈ HIMALAYAN RAIN SHADOW

THE LODGING HOUSE IN KAG IS CALLED THE RED HOUSE, NO DOUBT because of the red-painted latticework on the windows to which thin cloth or paper is glued, to let the light through. I awake at dawn to a banging and a ferment stink that rises from the court below, where a small pregnant *dzo* (a yak-sired cow that provides milk as well as transport, the *dzo* is the fundamental animal here in the mountains) feeds from a tub of sour barley mash from which the strong *chang* or Tibetan beer, has been extracted.

Kagbeni is at the edge of the restricted area of Lo, and one cannot proceed north of this place without a permit. Foreigners must be accompanied by a "liaison officer" and also by Sherpas from an accredited tour company, in this case Tiger Mountain, which served us well twenty years ago on the journey to Dolpo. The *sirdar*, or head Sherpa, is Ang Temba, one of three who made it to the top of Everest in last year's all-Sherpa expedition (*National Geographic*, June 1992). The cook is Pemba Tsering, and his assistant is Sher Bahadur, called Sheri. Temba and Pemba are acquainted with Jangbu and Phu Tsering, who accompanied George Schaller and myself to the Crystal Mountain of Inner Dolpo in 1973. (Since then, Inner Dolpo, like Mustang, has mostly been closed to foreign travel.)

We are also accompanied by Laird's liaison officer, an affable young Brahman named Mr. Guru Bishnu Kafle, "an assistant sub-inspector of police" entrusted with the special duty of making sure that his party causes no episode at the "Chinese" border. The rest of the staff are from Lo Monthang. Ongdi, a porter, is in charge of Laird's cameras, Tashi and Bishnaduki own most of the horses, and two other Lobas (citizens of Lo) are along, unpaid, to watch over the remaining horses for the owners.

Unlike Loba women, whose one concession to Western dress are the flimsy sneakers that, along the river, have replaced the embroidered wool boots with soles of yak-hair twine, the men wear not only sneakers but pants and shirts and caps and jackets, though many still carry in their belts the ornate daggers of traditional dress with the scabbards shoved into hip pockets, and a few have traded for cast-off trekkers' clothes in Day-Glo colors, which contrast strangely with the warm natural dyes in the many-colored tough Tibetan carpeting under their saddles.

OPPOSITE ~ *The village of Chaili stands on the cliffs above the river. The main trail to Lo Monthang is visible winding up the side canyon to Samar.*

24

The sahibs, having breakfasted on tea and *tsampa* (barley porridge), descend to the river and walk north into Lo, then wait for the rest of the party to bring up the horses. These tough and sure-footed small Asian horses remind me of American Indian ponies, since the black manes and tails are braided with red and green ribbons that set off the bright colors of the saddle blankets. My own horse is Khyangba, or "Brownie," a dark brown gelding with a white star, black mane, and long black braided tail, with layers of bright blanket padding lashed across a small and punitive Tibetan saddle of wood and iron.

Counting the estimable Kafle, there are eleven men in all and fifteen horses. Besides tents, stove, and the like, we must carry provisions for ten days of exploration in eastern Lo, where the remote villages are small and far between.

We ride upriver on the silver stones past the village of Tangbe, then Chuksang, which is split in two by the alluvial fan of the Chuksang stream. Toward midday Chaili village appears, on a high cliff, and here the broad canyon narrows abruptly and disappears behind the cliff, leaving what looks like an impenetrable wall at the mouth of the upper gorge. The narrows is little more than a boy's stone throw, and a bridge has been built across the river. The trade route now climbs west toward the peaks before turning north again across the heads of the deep canyons, passing the main settlements of western Lo — Samar, Gelling, Gemi, Tsarang, Lo Monthang — and on into Tibet.

At Chaili we shall leave the trade route in favor of forging straight upriver through the upper gorge. Until five years ago, when an underground glacial lake, so it is thought, burst through the cliffs near the river's source and rushed downriver, this narrow twenty-mile ravine with sheer walls up to two thousand feet high had been impassable. Then the great flood, and a lesser one two years ago, scoured out centuries of rock debris, and a few Loba have since ventured through on horses. Laird heard about this awesome gorge last autumn on his first visit to Lo, and this spring became the first foreigner to try it. Even now, in these last days of low water, one must crisscross the gray torrent a hundred times where it curls around the canyon's twisted corners. By the time we come back south in early June, the ice and snow melt farther north will have raised the flood and it will no longer be passable, even on horseback.

To a rock pinnacle at the entrance of the canyon flies a blue rock thrush, crowned with silver in this desert sun. Though it is singing, I cannot hear it in the mounting wind, only the wistful ringing of the horses' bells as they move in a long line into the canyon, where the blue sky narrows to mere hope of light, high overhead. The file of horses fords the river at the first bend, where the torrent has carved a bouldered channel under the sheer wall.

Unless they start through the ravine at daybreak and make it out of the far end before dark, the Loba have no liking for the gorge route, since there is little forage for the horses on the few sand benches

saligrams, offered by travellers on the pass above Tey

where camp can be made above the flood. Also, the gorge route, though much shorter, is harder on the animals, since the riverbed is paved with rolling cobbles, and the horses, up to their chests in water, must plunge across the flow over and over. Under such high walls, in this narrow place, the dark comes early, and anyway, these men, whose thoughts are filled with demons, so cheerful about cold and discomfort, mistrust wild places without people or houses. "This isn't a human place," the Loba say. This is not a place where man belongs. Like the horses, they stay bunched up close.

◈ SALIGRAMS

YEARS AGO AT BENI BAZAAR, ON THE KALI GANDAKI SOUTH OF Dhaulagiri, a young boy sold to me for about ten cents a smoothed black river stone containing the spiral form of a marine fossil — an ammonite already one hundred million years old when, fifty million years ago, the upthrust of these mountains, inch by inch, lifted it from the sea floor of the Eocene. Three times more ancient than the peaks themselves, the beautiful saligrams, so mysterious and universal in their spiral shape, are said by the Hindus who find them down the river to be earthly manifestations of Great Vishnu, Preserver of all Life. Thus the saligrams are sacred, and the river, too.

This canyon turns out to be a place of saligrams, which look like roc eggs — strange roundish rocks of a dull velvety black that stand out among the grays and silvers of the river. Coming across one, a local man will hurl it against a boulder to expose the fossil inside, usually shattering the fossil in the process. "It is not cooked," or "It is not ready to come out," they say, when one is ruined.

One of the two Lobas named Karma has a geologist's small pick and tries to free his saligrams more subtly, so that the two halves of the split stone make a fit, but even this man makes a botch of most of them. "There are a lot more around," Karma observes, dropping the pieces, "when the water looks black." Laird and I smiled at this idea, but as we were to learn, he was not wrong. Often the discarded fragments are quite beautiful, though my own favorites are the spirals naturally exposed in the tumble of the current and worn silk smooth, cool to the hand.

The horses splash across the fan of a small brook that falls down through a steep cut from the town of Samar, high up on the mesas to the west — all that is left, after irrigation, of the Samar Khola. Just beyond, we make our camp on a broad bench under the long arch of an overhang, setting up tents against the wind that has driven us like fugitives up the canyon.

The wind dies slowly after dusk, and the fiery stars that shine on lands as yet unshrouded by the filth of man appear in the blue-black firmament above. I go to sleep to the rushing of the river. Though the bench is a few feet above water level, one would not care to find oneself in this long canyon in a flash flood, but the seasons are steadfast in the Himalayan rain shadow and do not often take one by surprise. The water will rise a little every day, according to ice melt in the glaciers, but so far there are only whisperings of monsoon rain.

OPPOSITE ~ *manmade caves in the eroded cliffs near Yara*

Trangmar takes its name from these cliffs. The prayer wall in front is said to be the longest in Nepal and is studded with stones carved with mantras.

◈ THE THREE TREASURES

THE CAMP RISES TOWARD FIVE A.M. WITH THE FIRST LIGHT ON THE rim, far overhead, and Pemba and Sheri bring tea and *tsampa,* the farina made from roasted barley ground to flour that is the foundation of the Tibetan diet.

In the old canyon, the song of the plumbeous redstart is a thread of silver in the gray of the river's running. On the river edge lies a saligram inlaid with gold. Beyond this gorge we shall leave the Kali Gandaki and head up a side canyon into eastern Lo, making our way north across the canyons and plateaus before returning west in a fortnight's time to Lo Monthang.

A cold north wind out of Tibet descends the canyon. In a few hours, the Lobas say, this wind will die, and after a brief mid-morning stillness, the great wind from the south will come, to scour and batter the landscape until dusk.

The iron hoofs ring under the overhanging rocks, but the ringing is borne off by the torrent as the horses plod and stumble up the narrow canyon. Boots wet and cold from frequent crossings, we are grateful for the shafts of sun that find their way down to the few open bends. At a dark narrows, an overhanging mass of rock descends so low that it forms a tunnel in the canyon, a twisted grotto scarcely wide enough for the pack horses. Surely this place would dismay travellers who sought to venture southward through the canyon, and one must admire the courage of the first to venture in and keep on going.

Then, like portals to the northern kingdom, the soaring walls burst wide into open canyon bathed in morning sun, and the warm banks are frequented by birds that were mostly missing from the gorge — pied wagtails and black redstarts, white-capped river chats, and everywhere, up and down the walls, crag martins and the blue-barred rock pigeons, so similar and yet so wary, wild, and swift compared to their domesticated soiled descendants in the ravines of cities the world over.

North of the gorge, the Gelling Khola descends from the plateaus above. Unlike the Samar, the Gelling is dry, since all of its flow has been channeled off to irrigate the village fields on the west mesas somewhere up behind the river walls. At the confluence lie stone corrals or *ghots* used by the herdsmen, set about with dozens upon dozens of small chortens, three or four stacked rocks smeared with red clay,

like a cockeyed crowd of celebrants of the earth's elements. To Buddhist scholars, the stacked rocks, like the stupas or chortens, represent variously the elements — earth, water, air, and fire — or the Three Treasures — Buddha, Dharma, Sangha — but to the local people the small figures are the very body of the Buddha, like the mountains and rivers, the bird voices and saligrams, the goat and sheep dung turning to powder on these rocks, to be carried away to the Ganges plain as the river rises.

The deep ravine has given way to a broad and sunwashed desert riverbed of Central Asia, across which, watched by the dread mountain deities in the black peaks on the sky, the men and horses, like a file of ants, wander back and forth across the shining silver stream, crossing deep shadows beneath wind-eroded cliffs, infinitely transient and minute in such immensity, utterly lost in so much earth and air. There is no sound nor even silence, no vapor trail nor hum of distant road, no glint nor scar nor smallest trace of unnatural detritus anywhere across the miles and miles of silver riverbed. Since leaving Jomsom, we have heard no motor, nor anything except the cry of birds, the click of hooves and quiet blowing of the horses, the bells, the yells and whistles of the hostlers, the silent echo in the wake of an ancient boulder that loses its hold on its sandstone niche of fifty million years and tumbles down the wind-worn walls with distant thunder. We have met no man nor seen his trace, only the dried dung of goats and horses and the old camp fire at the *ghot* by Gelling Khola.

On a river bend is a small grove of fifteen-foot trees — *thanq-za-ra*, Ongdi calls them — one of the very few wild groves to be seen in Lo. This shelter has been found by a small quick band of leaf warblers, descended like petals from the sky to the only green place in this pale sere canyon.

Swirling clouds have followed the wind of midday from the south, but these are mere weak forays of the monsoon. Here in Lo, the true bad weather comes in high from the northwest, so says Tom Laird, to descend like a black hand upon the mountains.

Having already visited the main trade route settlements in western Lo (which I shall pass through in any case on my return journey), Laird is anxious to explore the side valleys and far-off hamlets on the remote eastern side of this central valley, and that afternoon, we leave the Kali Gandaki, turning up a large tributary stream called Tange Khola. On both sides are soft conglomerates of marine sands, clay, and rock deposits eroded off the higher mountains and cut through by the river, which (like the saligrams) is ages older than the peaks.

manmade caves of mysterious origin in the cliffs of Trangmar

A few miles upriver, in high cliffs, are more of the mysterious cliff dwellings already noticed near the Gelling Khola. These caves have astonished the few visitors to Lo. As Dr. Tucci has pointed out, whole settlements in West Tibet were cave villages until quite recently, and it is assumed that these were villages of early Lobas, whose hermit monks later used them as retreats. But certain authorities now speculate that some, at least, were neolithic sites of early man from the centuries when water was still plentiful, and these mountains still forested and full of game, and even the deserts to the north were fertile plains.

Red chortens and green fields of Tange village appear above the river cliffs on a north bend. The wind is rising, with snow mists on the peaks to the south and east, and a wind roar resounds from the carved pinnacles high overhead as we climb up slowly from the river. At the west end of Tange are the remains of a village several centuries old, to judge from the worn nubs of walls and chortens. Skeletal villages are common in this landscape, suggesting that in early times, the land supported many more people than it does today.

The barley fields are watered from above by a small canal — perhaps two feet across, six inches deep — led down from a small pond at the west end the village, and replenished by an upper aqueduct that comes from somewhere higher in the canyons. Along this ditch grow copious wild roses, a purple vetch, and a few red-barked cherry trees — more plant life than we have come across anywhere north of the Himalaya. The elevation cannot be more than 10,000 feet, low enough so that the barley crop, as at Kagbeni, can be augmented by a second crop of buckwheat.

Rock buntings and impeyan pheasant. At Tange the rock pigeons of the canyons are displaced by the hill pigeon, a paler form with flashing white rump and white band on the tail. (Farther north we shall see another sibling species, the snow pigeon.) To the top of the huge east entrance chorten flies a *grandala*, a large bright indigo bird, black-winged. This chorten has delicate frescoes on the ceiling of its passageway and a host of lesser chortens in attendance, and as at Kagbeni, all are freshly painted for the Buddha's birthday.

Big black-and-brindle mastiffs guard most of the twenty-five-odd households, and during the day all but the very old and young among these animals are chained. The sight of a gargling mastiff, twisting and strangling on its chain in desperate instinct to tear him into pieces, is the customary welcome to the stranger, who is quite content, nevertheless, to be sleeping behind walls, since the flapping of tents can wear the nerves in such a wind. We stay in the house of Sarme-la, whose husband is away up in the mountains, tending his herds. "Yaks need no tending," smiles this fetching person, in apparent reference to wolf and snow leopard, "but the others do."

Like most Lo houses, this one is constructed around a central light shaft, with stalls for animals on the ground level and one or two stories built above. The low wood doors and low-ceilinged windowless rooms with sapling cross beams and hard clay floors are characteristic of the Buddhist Himalaya. On the flat roof, between blowing prayer flags and shrines to the protective deities, are stacked the wood and drying brush and twigs that kindle the cooking fires in the mud stoves below. We are lodged without much fuss in the family chapel, with its simple altar, where villagers are invited to come look at us.

The people here are handsome even by trans-Himalayan standards. In their poor European dress, the men seem small and nondescript, but the women's oriental delicacy combined with a wild open Tatar vigor can be breathtaking. Long black cloaks — the traditional *chuba* — bound around by homespun belt and aprons of bright-dyed twists of red, green, blue, and fire-colored wool and set off by necklaces of coralline and turquoise — such finery suits their black hair and ruddy color to perfection. Some of the older women and a few infants wear the traditional hard-wool shoes, and one woman carries the old-time wooden back rack, like an upside-down chair, in which she bears her large brass flagon full of water.

Water is too precious (and too heavy) to be used for washing, and the people are marvelously soiled — half of one boy's face is crusted with black scabs from impacted dust. Everything here is constructed out of mud, from the sun-dried mud bricks of the house walls (sometimes the mud walls are moulded between boards, which are later removed) to the hard floor of compacted gritty dust, and also the cooking fuel is dung, which dries to a fine dust suited perfectly to blackening the pores. The women's hands are black right up the arms, and stay that way, since the bathless life is considered beneficial to one's health.

In the late afternoon a cold wind brings light rain — "Good for these people," says sad-faced Karma Two, looking reproachfully toward the mountains, "but hard for us travellers."

⬚ TRACK OF JACKAL, PRINT OF SNOWCOCK

THIS MORNING THERE IS A LIGHT DUSTING OF SNOW ON THE mountains all around, but the sky is clear again, all the world shining. Climbing up to the high chortens at the east end of Tange, above the confluence of river forks, Laird and I are rushed by a silent mastiff there to guard the herd, and Tom yells at me to grab a rock. Confronted by hominid threat display, the black dog barks and growls but keeps its distance.

A trail leads to a high mountain pass between Tange and Tey, a village on another tributary some miles to the north, and we set off up the northern fork of Tange Khola, which rushes along in its canyon well below. Between trail and torrent is a sparkling ditch, diverted from the upper stream, that rounds the mountain and descends into Tange's little manmade pond, which waters the stone-walled terrace fields below.

Track of jackal, print of snowcock.

These mountainsides have a brown-black cast very different from anything we have encountered, a very fine dark dusty soil, almost black in places, that climbs in rolling hills like dunes to a rim of extraordinary pinnacles, like a company of black demons on the north horizon. The climb is steep, and the tough small horses tire, and here and there we rest them, or get off and walk. Off to the west, on the far side of the Kali Gandaki, the high passes through the mountains to Dolpo may be seen, and to the south, the north face of Dhaulagiri and the vast snowfields of Annapurna rise gradually from behind the lesser peaks. Between them, plunging out of sight into its own abyss, the awesome gorge that ruptures the white ice wall is purple-gray in a dark smoky mist of its own emptiness. Beyond, going away forever to the south, is the blue sky of the subcontinent — Nepal and India.

And it is now that the first lammergeiers, two together, draw near in their slow motionless arcs to scan our string of horses, and a third appears, far up the eastern mountainside toward those sentry pinnacles. At eye level and below, the great raptors turn and turn without one wingbeat, their golden heads catching the sun each time they wheel.

Throughout the ascent we notice scattered saligrams. Ongdi claims that somewhere in the Tey watershed, where we are headed, is the main source of saligrams in the Kali Gandaki, "a saligram mine" that is worked by the Tey people. Even so, we are unprepared for the chorten at the pass, which is crowded with saligrams of exceptional size and quality — one of them "the finest I have ever seen!" exclaims Tom Laird. Restraining the impulse to pilfer these sacred stones placed here in offering, we marvel at the piety of folk who heap such treasure on a high mountain pass.

Lo's sacred mountain Dhungmara Himal is rising in the west, beyond an emptiness among the peaks where lies Lo Monthang's plain; its glacier is the source of the Kali Gandaki. Our trail is north toward the mountains of Tibet, which come into view as the farthest ridge on the horizon. Escorted by snow finches in bounding flight, like blowing papers, we cross the pass and start the descent toward Tey, a green patch on the cliff edge, far below. And almost at once, set out before us, is the explanation of why so many saligrams lie on that chorten, and why the Tey Khola is so renowned. A tumultuous landslide of black soil hundreds of yards across and descending thousands of feet down toward the river is fairly littered with these fossils, whole ones and in pieces, small and large — by far the largest we have ever found. Even Ongdi and Kafle, who are with us, can scarcely believe what they are seeing.

This slipping mountainside of fine black soil at 13,000 feet can be nothing but pure sediment of the sea floor of the Jurassic Period, one hundred and sixty million years ago, now dried to black dust in the high clear air of the Central Asian desert. And these ammonite fossils at our feet lay in the abyssal deposit that over the ages was lifted by inches from the depths, thousands of feet into the mountain sun and the blue sky. What we discover is that many if not most are of a brown-gold color and so brittle that some actually crumble in the hand. Therefore it appears that relatively few — perhaps only the black ones, much less common here — survive the long slow journey down the mountainside to the Tey Khola, to be tumbled and turned down the ravines to the great Gandaki, which carries the most obdurate survivors all the way south to the southern plains and even, perhaps, over the centuries, back to the Indian Ocean from which they came. That idea stirs me! And of these few, but a few are ever found, and of those few, but a few are opened cleanly, either by man or by the river — hence the high value of the "perfect" saligram in Kathmandu.

We stuff packs and pockets and continue down the mountain to Tey village, where we are greeted by astonished, friendly children who bow to us in awe, whispering *"namaste"* in greeting. (*Namaste* has been translated: "I honor the place in you that is light-filled and universal, where if you are in that place in you and I am in that place in me, there is only one of us.") We are the first foreigners the people can remember except for two men who came through here about six years ago — illegal travellers avoiding the main towns along the trading route, in Laird's opinion, since no foreigners were admitted at that time, and no permits for this wilder country east of the Kali Gandaki are being issued even today.

Most of the villagers are collected around the irrigation pond, where a man is shovelling mud into deep baskets that are then lifted to the women's backs and secured by tump line to their foreheads. The women lug the wet mud to higher ground where it is packed into a wooden mold, which is then overturned, and the wet mud bricks set out to dry until the time that they are used in the new house. Like the construction and maintenance of irrigation channels — though not the tending of the fields — the labor is communal, and the workers' meals, provided by the owner of the house, are the only pay.

In Tey village, which has twenty-one households and not much more than one hundred people, a woman with a backstrap loom is weaving yak wool for making a nomad tent. Beside her, another spins wool into thread, the upright spindle turning in a bowl of beaten copper. Just below, a horse is being fed a basket of fresh weeds culled by the old people and children from the sparse new wheat, for spring comes late at this altitude (above 12,000 feet) and forage is still scarce. Here in Tey, there is only enough warm weather to produce a single crop each year, and wheat is preferred to buckwheat or barley. But the single crop does not leave enough winter straw to feed the stock, and the barley straw scattered along the Tange trail comes from yak loads bartered for by the Tey people.

The people complain that too many blue sheep are damaging the grazing for their domestic animals, and Laird asks how many *na* there are in the high pastureland of Damodar Kunda, to the east. "How the hell do we know?" a man laughed at him. "Who would count them?" Another man complained that snow leopards come frequently and raid the stock, and since the people have no guns, the leopards must be driven off with rocks. Asked if they'd taken any skins, the first man made everyone laugh by saying, "No! The snow leopards still have them!"

THE PRECARIOUSNESS OF LIFE

LAST NIGHT WE CAMPED IN THE MUD ROOMS OF THE SCHOOL, SINCE no household in Tey is prepared for visitors. The night was cold, very close to freezing, and this morning it is overcast. Soon it is snowing. Afternoon clouds and sometimes rain are normal in the monsoon season, but dark morning weather can mean worse to come at the higher altitudes farther north. However, the snow desists as we trek down the steep side of the Tey valley, traversing ugly tumulus ravines, starting up rose finches, a Tibetan hare. Across the deep valley, more caves appear, impossibly high up in the pinnacles. The Tey folk say that in olden days, their people inhabited these cliff houses, but the steps and tunnels that gave access to them are long since worn away in the soft rock. At least one was occupied by a Buddhist monk, to judge from traces of red ochre that can be made out through binoculars, also a wall painting of a chorten and twin lotus flowers, in a motif that Laird believes to be at least two centuries old.

Farther down, the path crosses what looks like a black avalanche but is, in fact, abyssal muck — the slide of ocean sediment that we saw yesterday — flowing slowly down a mountainside perhaps a thousand miles from the nearest sea. All the way down, saligrams are common. The black flow falls away and disappears over the cliffs, down to the river.

Along this *khola,* or river, the folk of the Kali Gandaki villages harvest saligrams that the Tey people regard as theirs — which may, indeed, have been the reason that they settled up above, since their high plateau is small and poor and their life hard, and this valley which everyone agrees is the main source of saligrams is the most steep, dark, and forbidding we have come across. The canyon walls are tortured by long ages of twisting and collapse, and the riverbed is a tumult of steep-sided rock benches and large boulders that will demand the utmost from the horses. The Loba say that the flow of the black muck in the monsoon blocks up Tey Khola, building up a wall of water which eventually bursts the dam and scours out the whole canyon, changing the conformation of the bottom, leaving deep gullies. Yet saligrams are abundant on the river margins, and all of them are black. As predicted, the brown ones do not make it down even this far.

On the north wall, some distance down this river, is a faint trail one of the Karmas claims he has seen horses descend. Presumably the trail zigzags up and over the cliff and continues north across the mesas to the next watershed, eliminating the need to return to the Kali Gandaki. At the foot of this trail, our small caravan divides, for we are lightening the loads and sending six horses and several of the men down to the Gandaki and west to Lo Monthang; Bishnaduki will return to us in a few days with some hay for the remaining horses, for there is little forage at these altitudes in May, and the two villages had none to spare after the winter. With no more river crossings, only streams, the Sherpas will continue north on foot, together with Ongdi and Tashi and two pack horses, while the Americans and their liaison officer Mr. Kafle will remain mounted as before.

The climb traces the old thin shadow of a trail that wanders fitfully up the valley side. Some of the path is very loose and all of it is steep, and the horses, tired from slipping and stumbling down the rough Tey Khola, must be rested frequently and, in places, led. Near the rim it passes through a cluster of large boulders, emerging at last on a high lonesome mesa that slopes gradually west toward the main river. In this exposed place, the big wind from the Himalaya has reduced the caragana bushes to small tight round nubs, with all the yellow florets on the northern side.

There is still some restless weather in the west, looming over the trail that leads up the ravines from the Kali Gandaki toward Dolpo, and a different weather in the south, where thick monsoon clouds are crowding through the Himalayan portal. From the look of it, it must be snowing on the ridges above Kagbeni and Jomsom, and the snow extends across the western mountains. Far away on the mesas on the far side of the Kali Gandaki can be seen the green fields of Tsarang, along the cliff edge of the Tsarang Khola.

Near the rim of the Luri canyon, the horses are left untended on the mesa while we explore the cliff edge, which falls off abruptly into the strange fluted pinnacles of wind erosion. The pinnacles descend a thousand feet into the river, and just opposite, as if placed there for the view, lies the village known as Yara. Working the air currents below the rim is a huge creamy-buff vulture, the Himalayan griffon, together with crag martins, red-billed choughs, and the *gorak,* or raven.

A mile away over the mesa, the untethered horses stand motionless, facing the wind. I am ever more fond of Khyang-ba, who has learned to stand motionless while I study birds through my binoculars, and who spared me serious injury this morning in the Tey Khola. A fine saligram passing close to his hooves inspired me to swing too quickly from the saddle, startling the horse and causing him to jump out sideways before my boot was free of the small stirrup. (Tom Laird, who has suffered this mishap twice — Kafle has, too — had warned me about it before we started out.) I was slammed down hard on my back upon large stones, and as I lay half-stunned, trying to twist my foot free, I held my breath in fear Khyang-ba would bolt, bouncing my head along among the stones. Tom Laird, not ordinarily an agile man, was out of his saddle in an instant, and the foot came free as he arrived, but the horse, after its first scare, stood still and calm throughout all the commotion.

We return along the rimrock to the horses and ride upriver on the mesa to the point where a trail descends into the canyon. Crossing the river and climbing again to Yara village, we are met on the path by Pemu Nu, a Kagyu lama in charge of Luri Gompa, who will accompany us on our visit there tomorrow.

By now it is late, and we ride out of Yara and proceed upriver a few miles to Ghara, a small poor village with meager gardens. But the people if not the terrible chained dogs are as open and cheerful and resolutely filthy as they are every place else, and though they stare and touch and crowd into every space, make us feel welcome. We are lodged in a private house hastily prepared for the occasion. While pleasant enough and well appointed with old brass-bound wooden butter churns and other artifacts, the house lacks the usual toilet slot in the upper floor, since the folk of Ghara visit a ditch outside the walls when on this errand (human excrement is mixed with dung from the adjoining stalls and spread upon the fields).

The people are not sophisticated — we watch our host paint iodine on his sprained hand — and some are wary of Laird's camera. Like many traditional people, not unnaturally, they fear that something is being taken from them, that in some way their own self or spirit is being stolen. "We don't know what happens to those pictures," one woman calls, backing through her door. "Perhaps they are just put away some place, or become dirty, or are lost." Her house, like most houses in Lo, has a dead hare in a demon-trap over the door (not the same as the protective *shrungma* deities kept in the house or on its roof or sometimes on a ridge high above the village). In these mountains the inhabitants are overwhelmed by the precariousness of life and the need to placate the dread demons of the peaks and swift cold torrents and almighty weathers.

While at Ghara we talked with two herders, just arrived, who were bringing a flock of fine black-and-white goats south from Tibet for trade at Muktinath. Apparently they had journeyed out of "China" through the remote northern valley where we were headed. Tashi and Karma, who talked with them, reported their exciting conversation to the three Sherpas, who assumed we had also been told the news until they discovered a few days later that we hadn't.

◈ SILENT MOUNTAINS

FROM THE ROOFS OF GHARA ON A BRIGHT MOUNTAIN MORNING, A VAST extent of the Himalaya lies in view, with fresh snow on the mountains westward, on the Dolpo border. A man brings a spotted dove he has trapped on his own roof this morning, a pretty vinaceous bird with a broad black collar spotted white that I am surprised to encounter at this altitude — according to Laird, close to 13,000 feet.

The Luri Monastery lies up the valley a few miles, past a tiny hamlet known as Kete. Due to the constant wind erosion, much of it has fallen or been worn away from its pinnacles above the river, so much so that it is all but hidden. One rounds the base of an eroded column and there it is, far overhead, a small red building on the desert sky. But for its fire color and white prayer flags, one might miss it entirely. Under the gompa are old caves occupied formerly by hermit monks. All around this central building perched so precariously among the pinnacles, the cave rooms and corridors and ladder shafts have been laid open to the wind.

The ascent to Luri is by way of a steep path that crosses a crevasse between pinnacles by sapling bridge and climbs once more to the ledge and gompa door, where the stone and wood is worn to a hard shine. Behind the door, all that is left of the first floor is the old kitchen, from which one climbs up by log ladder through the trap door above. Here the walls are decorated with garish, rather recent Buddha figures which do not prepare the visitor for the ancient altar room within. This Lha-kang (literally, "God House"), or religious room or chapel, is dark and windowless as a cave, but with torches the gold faces of ancient Buddha figures become visible, gleaming dully in the shadows of a soot-blackened "sky" or canopy of Chinese gold-and-silver silk brocade. To the left of the altar, by the drum, is a wood box lined with homespun rugs in which the lama sits in meditation. The custodian from Ghara lights the butter candles, offers water in brass bowls, burns sprigs of juniper as purifying incense.

Astonishing as this dark chapel seems in such a place, it is not the spiritual or artistic heart of Luri, which lies concealed behind a low narrow door in the blackness on the left side of the altar. Here another sacred room — this one is round — contains a superb round chorten of the 15th century, eight feet in diameter, perhaps fifteen feet high, filling the small room so completely that only a narrow space is left for circumambulation. A very small square window looks out over the mountains, but lanterns are needed to study the exquisite line and detail of the ancient paintings, not only the murals on the walls and ceilings but the paintings on the polished-plaster surface of the chorten, all of them largely intact and only slightly faded, since the room is dark.

Unlike most Buddhist shrines in Lo, Luri is not a Sakya temple but one affiliated with the Kagyu sect, since the great Kagyu teachers Tilopa and Naropa and Marpa are all here. The Sakyamuni Buddha and Chenrezig figures are true masterpieces, beyond comparison with anything in Mustang, says Tom Laird, except for two painted mandalas on the walls of the Champa (Maitreya) temple in Lo Monthang. Experts who have seen Laird's photographs say that portraits of such great age in this fluid style do not exist anywhere outside of Lo. Even before the 1950s, when the Chinese destroyed most of its religious art, Tibet had few cave chortens surrounded by paintings, and today this one at Luri is among the last.

I climb a ladder to another story, mostly sunny terrace, where I sit quiet, gazing away over the mountains. At first I pay close attention to the higher slopes in hope of seeing browsing animals — blue sheep or *tahr* — but soon I put down my binoculars and regulate my breath and lose myself in peaceful meditation. Soon Lama Pema Nu appears, poking the handsome head of an American Indian up through the floor with a grand smile, then climbing up to sit beside me, saying nothing. Though we cannot speak, we are content in the sun and silence, listening to sweet songs of the great rose finch and black redstart that have replaced man as inhabitants of the gompa.

Pema Nu did his own retreat here as a youth, spending three years, three months, and three days in one of the tower caves below the gompa. His father and grandfather were lamas here before him, and during their lifetimes the monastery was still active. It was much bigger then, he says, but the wind has worn away most of the rooms and caves, and one day Luri will be no more than a set of hollowed caves high on the wall, as inaccessible as the ancient monastery site across the gorge.

In other days there were three large monasteries in these river cliffs, but Luri is the only one in which the sacred rooms are still intact, and one of the very last of the old cave monasteries in Lo (and Tibet). Alas, there is no money in the kingdom to maintain it, or even to preserve the masterpieces in the gompa, which cannot be removed. Without interest and help from the outside world, it will not be long before Luri's pinnacles erode around it, and this precious place in the rock and sky crumbles away down this steep slope into the rivers.

For a few hours after the rest have gone, I remain by the chorten at the foot of the path, in the spell of that small red temple overhead, the prayer flags, birds, the liberating emptiness of the silent mountains all around, whirling through time.

▨ SAO GOMPA

MAY 22

THE MASTIFF CHAINED BY THE ENTRANCE TO OUR HOUSE HAS BEEN thrown an entire kid (that is to say, a baby goat), which it has stripped naked of its hide and gnawed but left uneaten. The stiff small carcass, stuck with dung and straw, is still between its paws early next morning when we depart, walking with Ongdi up the hill to await the horses.

Bandy-legged Ongdi is poor and without prospects, ordered around by everybody else, although they like him. Until 1956, when serfdom in Lo was formally abolished, he had no rights whatever in the world, and he still retains much of the serf mentality seen in the Lobas; he once got down and tried to kiss Laird's feet after the gift of a pair of shoes, an act which would be unimaginable among the Sherpas. However, he is sly and observant and manages quite well. Unlike the others (they are envious) Ongdi got drunk and made love last night. "I knew her when she was younger, now she is old, but she can't help that — what are you going to do?" He laughs a little, generous and cynical, teasing us about the "bed tea" brought each morning to our sleeping bags by our good Sherpas. "That woman said she would bring me my tea up here on the hill," he grumbled, peering comically about him. "Where do you suppose she's got to now?"

Ongdi and his paramour of the evening previous had discussed the Khampa guerrillas from east Tibet who harassed the Chinese for many years from their camps here in Lo, how they raided and pillaged all these villages, raping the women and girls caught in the fields — they talked of these events while making love, Ongdi reflected, smoking his cigarette in the sun. "We worked and talked, worked and talked," he said.

The Khampa horsemen from east Tibet were renowned brigands even in the days of the first European traders on the Silk Route, but their patriotism and sacrifice in the cause of their country's liberation from the Chinese can scarcely be questioned. Despite the protests of Nepal, which was trying to stay neutral, logistical support in this vain hope of "liberation" was provided by the American CIA, in one of the most obscure campaigns of the Cold War. In the early '70s, when the United States sought rapprochement with the Red Chinese, the Chinese made it a condition that the U.S. withdraw its covert support for the Khampa, and the funds were cut off almost overnight. Since they could not go home, the Khampas began to support themselves with Buddhist treasures from the monasteries, which were sold off to rich Loba and Tibetans as well as to Western art collectors in Kathmandu. Within the year, under pressure from the Red Chinese or the Americans, or both, Nepal sent its soldiers into Lo to clear the last Khampa from the region.

Besides temple treasures, the Khampa sold valuable zi — small tubular black stones with curious markings that "come from the lightning and fall on the mountains," Ongdi explained. (The rare zi stones have been copiously reproduced in the glass factories of Europe and sold as holy stones to unsuspecting peasants, who wear them on necklaces with their bits of poor silver and turquoise.) "If it had only been my karma to have found a zi stone, my life would have been very different. But, oh, poor pubic hair, me! My karma is to smoke cigarettes and drink *chang* and fork over every penny that I make to my old mother!"

We ride up the north face of the valley. From the upper trail, we can see Ghara's irrigation pond and near it a rare grove of juniper, left uncut beside old monastery ruins. Higher up, an hour above the village, an old man seeking fodder for his cow is chopping the last low hard patch of green scrub from the steep mountainside, and I am reminded of a man seen yesterday who was singeing the needles off juniper branches which were then pulled into strips by his wife and children. This hard and bitter juniper is also cattle fodder, and observing such practices makes one wonder how much man and his animals are responsible for the desert condition of this landscape, which seems to carry more vegetation at high altitudes, far from the villages, than at more moderate elevations. Higher still are the first cushion plants, round balls of lichen with tiny orange-white florets that are already gone from some valleys of east Nepal, Ang Temba says, hacked from the bare ground for fodder as well as for fuel for the many tourist inns.

From the pass above Ghara at 14,000 feet can be seen the open plains of western Lo, and even the villages of Tringar and Phuwo, north of Lo Monthang, and Kechar Dzong, the ruined 14th-century fort that overlooks that valley.

The wind is still out of the north. The track climbs gradually from the Ghara pass across a high plateau, bare haunt of larks. Despite the altitude, there is more vegetation here in this remote cold country than can be found anywhere on the warm valley sides, with plentiful yellow-flowered caragana and the lavender-white honeysuckle called lonicera and even an occasional small juniper.

The trail descends once more to Amekak, not a village but a simple *ghot* or stock corral, by a mountain brook from which a caravan of laden yaks is setting out for the Kali Gandaki with great swaying side loads of goat dung fuel. Our animals drink at the little stream and then we are climbing the far side, past a mastiff chained to a stone along the trail. She barks madly at our approach but quits and cringes as the horses draw near, being utterly at the mercy of hurled stones. She is there to warn the herdsmen of marauding wolves or leopards, Ongdi tells us.

This plateau is higher than the last — we estimate that we have travelled all this morning between 14,000 and 15,000 feet — and its northern rim is finally reached toward noon. On brown mesas to the north and east, strong dust devils are swirling. Before starting a formidable descent of two thousand feet or more into a deep canyon, we dismount and eat. One Karma brings gray and weighty discs of buckwheat bread and the other proffers a soiled plastic jug of *chang*, and in this way, keeping my own counsel, I celebrate my wonderful luck at finding myself on this eminence in the clear mountain air of Central Asia and the good fortune that permits me to lead such a wayward life. I am sixty-five years old this very day.

The canyon side is too steep and unstable to descend on horses, which must go down by a longer route than the one selected by the human beings. Ongdi, who prefers the horse trail, calls out to us not quite maliciously, "That short way is for goats!" And in fact, the horse route was quicker and easier than our own by quite a margin. The descent was treacherous indeed, all the more so since I had replaced my cleated boots with smooth-soled sneakers less liable to catch in the small stirrups. These were no match for the rough gullies and steep shale, the tortuous goat paths, ledges, and arroyos, and I was very glad to reach the bottom.

A few months ago, as the first Westerner allowed to visit Lo in thirty years, Tom Laird encountered in Lo Monthang a nomad herdsman from the Tibetan border region who told him about an extraordinary gompa in a remote high valley where no Westerners had ever been. Not unnaturally, he thought immediately of Shambhala, or Shangri-la — at any rate, he could not get the man's account out of his mind, and that valley is our ultimate destination. Though nomads are traditionally looked down upon as homeless vagrants, a boy in Ghara who stays in touch with these wandering people he refers to

46

as "my neighbors the nomads" had ridden out a day ahead to locate the nomad lama who was custodian of the remote gompa and might let us in. The Ghara boy would meet us at "Sao Gompa," as I shall call it, since for reasons that shall become quite clear, we have decided to disguise the real name of this remote valley as well as its location, pending some sort of protection for the place.

In the main canyon to which Sao Khola is tributary, riding along under great rock faces of clear pink and salmon — no longer sedimentary rock but a vibrant light-filled granite — there comes a sense of entering a new country and quite suddenly a strong buffet of wind. Just at that moment, the horse man Tashi looks back at us over his shoulder, then seems to turn and disappear into sheer wall. Closer, we see a portal in the rock that is so narrow — no more than thirty feet across between sheer walls — that the side canyon behind is all but hidden. Stranger still, the water in its stream, which has a good strong flow, is a glacial slate blue in color, the first and last such water we would see in Lo. Within the entrance, where the canyon opens out in a huge amphitheater before narrowing once more at the first bend, the river gravel is much finer than the rough cobbles of the main canyon, and we take advantage of the smooth packed surface to stretch the horses in a gallop across the bench to the first fording place.

A brief moment of exhilaration is quickly displaced by a vague sense of disquiet, for in this canyon is no sign of life, no plant, no bird. A half mile up on the west side, the canyon walls are stained a demonic orange by mineral springs that exude a weird shimmer of fire-colored fluid down the wall. Almost at once we are confronted by another bend that turns north into a gorge, and the Loba tell us we can go no farther due to steep waterfalls that choke the upper canyon. The alternative is to climb around the gorge, but the route of ascent looks shadowy and scarcely used and is, in any case, too steep for horses. Laird exclaims, "There *can't* be anything up there!" and indeed, the whole place seems so forbidding that, already tired by a long hard day of travel, we start the long tortuous ascent without much heart. The weather is ominous on the peaks, and my own spirits are not helped when, looking back, I see a black dog stretched taut on the gray gravel far below as if it had fallen from the sky. I am assured that the big dog isn't dead, merely guarding the camp gear of some herders who have taken their goats to higher altitudes — all the same, the emblematic shape, black on pale gray, is oddly disquieting. Higher up, I peer down again to see a huge round meteor of rock of unimaginable source wedged violently into the ravine — this, too, disturbs me.

American Indian friends have taught me that certain landscapes resonate with a dark power that warns the traveller to keep out or face death or injury, and possibly because I was so tired, this inhospitable canyon seemed to me that sort of place; for now one of the pack horses fell down with a screaming whinny, dumping its load, in a narrow upward defile through the big rocks.

We reached the top without further sign or incident, but having to stop often now to gasp for breath, I fell behind the others, enjoying this respite from the stress of human company. On foot, I followed a path up along the rim of the gorge choked by waterfalls, and eventually caught up with Mr. Kafle, kindly waiting to make sure I was still coming while taking his ease in the shade of a large boulder. Still oppressed by a strong sense of unknown power in this valley, I unwisely said as much to Kafle, but this light-hearted young Hindu had no idea what I might mean by this, and we put it aside at once as we walked along. And of course I did not understand myself. I could not speak about it sensibly since it was "unspeakable"; I only felt some sort of imminence, a little sinister.

Tom Laird, as well, had experienced powerful emanations from this place, but being much younger and more optimistic, had received them as sign of unimaginable and infinite possibilities — of "exploding horizons," as he put it, "as if we were no longer in a restricted or linear world."

Both of us, separately, were taken aback by the great size of the ancient weathered chorten that guarded the south pass of what seemed at first an empty desert canyon. For suddenly the gorge had opened out into a valley that broadened and softened as it ascended toward the north, the steep high cliffs at this south end giving way gradually to high greening hills, almost Elysian by comparison to the hard, lifeless country we had passed through.

Beyond the great chorten, a steep descent returned us to the valley floor at a point opposite a towering wall of rock, just above the boulder-blocked portals of the lower canyon. On this west side, the river bank was formed of stacks of beautiful gray slates as well as an outcropping of bitter salt, stamped around by the hooves of yaks and smaller animals, and up the valley a half mile was a high broad bench where we made camp. High overhead, among sharp pinnacles, could be seen worn flags and the small red structure of Sao Gompa.

Awaiting us are the boy from Ghara and two nomads in black cloaks and wool boots, sashes, daggers, and all. The nomads are the last men of Lo who still wear traditional costume. They have brought their herds down from the plateau to use the salt licks just above the falls and are camped at some old stone corrals just up the valley.

[➡ 58]

Horses with saddle carpets pass near the wind-scoured cliffs of Yara.

OPPOSITE ~ *the* Shrungma, *or Protector Deity, chapel at "Sao Khola"*

ABOVE ~ *A wall mural in the* Shrungma *chapel depicts the ritual coupling of deities.*

ABOVE ~ *mural depicting Buddha in Luri cave temple*   OPPOSITE ~ *Buddhist* siddhas, *depicted on the ceiling of Luri cave temple*

ABOVE ~ *Buddhist* siddhas   OPPOSITE ~ *The walls and chorten of the Luri cave temple were carved out of the cliff and painted.*

OPPOSITE ~ *Caves throughout Mustang once housed murals and statues, but today the paintings in Luri and the chapel in "Sao Khola" are nearly the only surviving examples of murals in caves.*   ABOVE ~ *Lama Pema Nu stands in the mouth of an abandoned cave at Luri.*

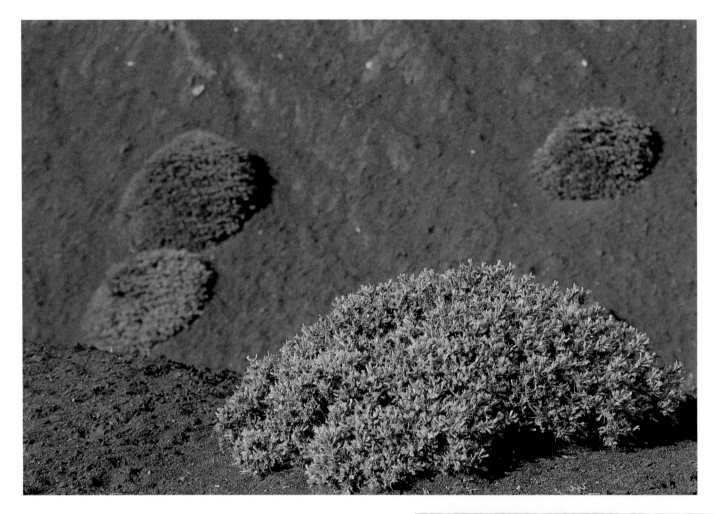

[The nomads] look like bandits with their swords tucked into their belts, their long unkempt hair, and their heavy wool and leather garments. Unsubmissive and restless, they are free masters of the vast silences on the roof of the world. They are the only people I envy: they are unfettered, serene in their inborn essential simplicity, ignorant of illusory architectures which time wears down and blows away like dust before the wind. As they wander through those immense spaces they seem to be suspended between heaven and earth.

— Giuseppe Tucci, *Journey to Mustang*[1]

THIS PAGE, TOP ~ *a caragana thorn bush in bloom near Tey*
ABOVE ~ *high meadow flower*
OPPOSITE ~ *Mineral-laden springs stain the cliffs near the entrance to the hidden valley of "Sao Khola."*

1 *Journey to Mustang,* 1952/Giuseppe Tucci. Kathmandu; Ratna Pustak Bhandar. 1977.

Lama Chotuk, in one of the abandoned cave temples of "Sao Khola"

Sao Gompa's custodian lama is Tenzing Chotuk, a small elfin-eared quick man of sudden smile and missing teeth and an air of absolute, ungovernable freedom. He wears wood prayer beads and a silver signet and a beautiful wood seal that is used, he says, for medicinal purposes, and in his sash a ceremonial horn made from a human thigh bone on which he offers a couple of cheerful toots. Pasum Duk, his brother-in-law, has a stunned, suspicious look and scarcely speaks. We take tea together out of the strong wind, sitting nomad-fashion on the striped horse blankets in the tent.

Sao Gompa is reached by a steep ravine that climbs perhaps two hundred feet, but even so, it is overwhelmed by that mighty face of rock across the river. The immanence of that looming mass, which towers over the gompa's highest pinnacle like some awesome threat of universal destruction, made the site still more inspiring to All-seeking monks than the site at Luri.

Lama Chotuk's wooden seal, used for medicinal purposes

Carved into the pinnacles and cliffs is a whole complex of chambers and caves on several levels, with kitchens and monks' cells and even a well-placed slot in a terrace floor with a long free-fall drop into the ravine. All of these chambers are set about with prayer flags on tall poles with triton shells and protector deities — prayer stones decked with yak and ram horns and even huge antlers of red deer. In one chamber is an entire stuffed yak calf with all the hair worn off; in another old mortars, butter churns, wicker baskets; in another old papier-mâché masks from the lama dances, becoming more grotesque each year as they sag and fall to pieces.

With heavy iron keys, the lama opens the red doors of the altar room, which is supported by four wood columns and measures about eighteen by eighteen feet — all that is left, he says, of a much larger chamber of twelve columns which collapsed some years ago. Behind the altar, where he offers incense and water, stand six superb golden Buddhas that Laird, a student of Tibetan Buddhist iconography, believes were made in 15th-century Lo Monthang. Fine as they are, these are only the remnants of a much larger temple treasure that, according to the nomads, was taken in the late sixties by the desperate Khampas.

For some reason — we don't understand quite why — Laird is able to cajole the lama into opening the small black chamber of the *shrungma* or guardian deities. Such a chamber is almost always present somewhere behind the walls of important temples, but not until today, after twenty years of study of religious sites in Nepal and Tibet, has he been permitted to see a *shrungma* chapel. "Perhaps it's because the gompa is no longer active, or because he has no experience with persuasive strangers. He says he has seen a few foreigners on trading journeys to Kagbeni, but that we are the first who have ever come into this valley." Very excited, voice gone high, Laird himself is uneasy about his triumph.

The small black chapel, reached by a narrow passage behind the altar, is crowded with hideous clay figures in fierce colors, including the blue figure of the Great Destroyer Mahakala and a warrior effigy with red face and pig snout, bearing antique Central Asian chain mail, shield, and helmet. On the walls all around are frescoed Tantric deities in costumes of elegant colors and exquisite detail, all of them in the *yab-yum* posture of upright copulation in which the female, embracing her furious lord, sits in or rather on his lap with her legs wrapped around his waist. Helping with camera lights, the frightened Tashi holds his collar over his mouth the whole time he is in this room, as a serf or low-caste person might in the presence of a great lama or king, to avoid giving offense to such dreadful beings.

Nomad, with his flocks, takes refuge in a cave.

The horse man Tashi is always curious and busy, repairing saddle girths, fashioning a nose ring for a yak out of bent juniper, agitating for a look through my binoculars. Now he has asked a question of Lama Chotuk, and the lama, leading him outside, draws a peculiar footprint in the dust. When Laird inquires, Tashi says, "The nomads say they saw these tracks this morning, down by the river." The lama then draws an improved footprint, saying that numbers of such prints had been made near the salt lick a few days earlier by a *mehti* — the problematic creature derided in the West as the yeti, or Abominable Snowman. And he drew forth from among his beads an amulet containing a braid of dark reddish-brown hair which he says was found by Pasum Duk, his brother-in-law, in a resting place made by the *mehti* in the cliff bank just above the falls. Twisted onto his prayer beads was a second braid, more faded, that he himself once found at higher altitudes where a *mehti* had been digging out a marmot's burrow.

Tashi, with his train of horses, descends the side canyon to Chaili.

Nodding, the taciturn Pasum Duk described how they had taken their animals down for salt and had come upon the prints and *mehti* fur. He supposed, he said, that the *shrungma* deities had sent the *mehti* down into this valley as a guardian, since the *mehti* were not known to come down so low. Plainly the uneasy nomads are associating its occurrence with the strangers' coming.

It is only now that the Lobas mention that the two herdsmen we had spoken with at Ghara, the ones bringing their black-and-white goats out of Tibet, had told the Lobas and our Sherpas, too, that coming south from the border through this valley, they had seen numerous *mehti* tracks near the salt licks in the Sao Khola — the same tracks, apparently, that these nomads had come across this morning. Tashi said he had assumed that our Sherpas had told us. "We never thought too much about it," Tashi explained. "We never thought that it would interest you."

FOLLOWING PAGES ~ *The nomads' grassy plateau is higher and east of these eroded canyons.*

print in the sandy riverbed said by the nomads to have been *left by a* mehti

The nomads, who arrived long after the goat traders had left, had known nothing of the earlier report but had made the discovery on their own. "They're just nomads," Tashi explained earnestly, "simpler than us village people, herding their animals all year up in those mountains." Tashi pointed at the rolling mountainsides of dark dull green that climbed from the head of the valley. "They didn't come here to talk about *mehtis.* They had no idea you would be interested in *mehtis.* They know nothing about foreigners. They say you are the first ever to come here!" He was all but wringing his hands. "*We* didn't know you were interested in *mehtis,*" poor Tashi pled, increasingly upset by Laird's annoyance that we had not been informed, "and if we didn't know, how could these poor nomads know who are even simpler than we are!"

Laird demanded that the lama lead us to those tracks at once. Like our own men, who do not question the existence of the *mehti* — Bishnaduki claims that he has seen it — Lama Chotuk was astonished by Tom's excitement. Though the lama had only seen one *mehti* in his life (Pasum Duk had seen two), the creature's tracks had been common this past year — and he rose and pointed — on those high pastures where the nomads pass most of their life; he was quite unwilling to rush down the river to the salt lick just to see those tracks again, all the more so since he felt uneasy about his animals. He and Pasum Duk, he said, should get back to the *ghot,* where their herds had been left in the care of two young girls.

---

the mehti, *as envisaged by the Tibetan painter Kaba Tarkay*

67

The light rain that had started a little earlier was turning to wet snow, and since it was already growing dark, I suggested that we defer this *mehti* expedition until we could see what we were looking at, the next morning. After all, several days had passed since we'd met those men at Ghara, so the putative prints could not be less than a week old, and, since then, the place had been heavily stomped over by yaks and goats and human beings — in the near dark, we might destroy the only good print left. But Laird was concerned that the snow might obliterate that last good print before he could get a photograph, and in moments we were headed off back down the river toward the gorge with the quick cat-like lama muttering crossly in the lead.

Scanning this way and that in the near dark, among the river stones, dung, and hoof prints, the lama finally located vague tracks in the hard black sand while the rest of us took care to move from rock to rock. The tracks were mostly worn and inconclusive, but one print was distinct and clear even in this blowing snow and failing light. It roughly resembled the foot of a small man of about the same size as the lama, whom I was rude enough to ask to press his own bare foot in the sand beside it. He complied cheerfully, even smiled, as he stripped off one yak-twine boot, having understood at once what I was up to.

As I had guessed, the lama's print was roughly the same size, and like the other, showed all five toes in a gradual curve. But the other print had a strange narrow heel and also a pronounced line behind the ball of the foot, just at the arch, which distinguished it at once from Homo sapiens.

A young nomad woman carries in a stubborn sheep for milking.

nomad woman of "Sao Khola" milking her sheep

Lama Chotuk showed us the scratched-out hollow in the black soil of the bank, well above the hoof prints, where in his opinion the *mehti* had made a resting place. It was here that his brother-in-law had found those strands of hair. Near this bed, a little higher up, I found a round print like a gorilla knuckle-print that the lama believed to be a *mehti* handprint. Saying this, he made a fist, pointing his knuckles down.

Tom Laird is ever more frustrated by dim light and failing batteries, not to speak of the wet snow in his lenses, but on the way back from the resting place, we discover that the one good track has been outlined by the blowing snow, which is not yet sticking to the bottom of the depression. Beside himself, he struggles to get what he hopes will be a decipherable picture.

Returning to camp in the near dark, we hear excited shouting and shrill cries from across the river. A snow leopard has killed two goats before being driven off by the shrieks and stones of the young women, and the nomads are much afraid for their other animals. In a moment, we go haring off again, this time upriver, but after a little ways come to our senses and return to camp. Too much is happening; we feel stunned and exhausted by so much strangeness and event, and our ears ring as if we were hallucinating.

nomad camp on the high plateau above "Sao Khola"

During supper, Tashi bursts into the tent and summons us outside. It has stopped snowing and the wind has died, and from the ravines across the river comes a high "yowp, yowp," like the last part of the "me-yow" of a house cat but a great deal louder and more resonant. At one point I draw Laird's attention to two separate cries, the "yowp-yowp" and a different one, farther away, that is more like the querulous "sao-sao" described so long ago to George Schaller and myself by the lama of the Crystal Monastery, in Dolpo.

A nomad family, with their yak-hair tent, encamped on the high plateau above "Sao Khola."

◈ *MEHTI* AND SNOW LEOPARD

I AM GLAD I'D MENTIONED THE TWO SEPARATE CRIES TO LAIRD WHEN Lama Chotuk turns up next morning with the news that at least two leopards (and perhaps three, to judge from the tracks they had found this morning) had ranged all night around their corral, trying to make off with the dead goats that the nomads had dragged in under the wall. The hungry cats had actually got their teeth into one carcass, only to be driven off by stones hurled by the boy from Ghara. Lama Chotuk declared it was a male, female, and young, though a female with one or two grown cubs seemed to me more likely. At any rate, the nomads are alarmed by such aggressive leopards (which, like the *mehti,* they associate with the coming of the foreigners) and intend to take their animals out of this valley this very morning. The young girls were too frightened to go out with the herds, and the hungry goats were penned in the corrals. "A single leopard can be driven off with rocks, but we do not expect to have to deal with two or three!" says Lama Chotuk, who blames the loss of the two goats on his own serious transgression in permitting strange men into the *shrungma* chapel.

The nomads have skinned out the goats and brought the carcasses to sell to us before departing. In the cold red neck of the carcass I inspected were two neat incisor penetrations. One goat will be reserved for leopard bait — Laird hopes to get a photograph tonight — and the other for the camp. As good Buddhists we do not kill goats, but neither do we discriminate against them. In short, there is no man here who will not help eat one.

By the time we reached the nomad camp at the north end of the valley, the young women and goats were already gone, and Pasum Duk and the lama were packing their few blankets and belongings on the least cantankerous of the huge yaks, which have nothing to fear from the likes of snow leopards. Glumly, Pasum Duk shows us the leopard pug marks, including a fine set made by a cat that had sneaked down a ravine and around the cliff base overlooking the corrals.

To the clang of heavy bells, Pasum Duk departs the valley, goading his red-tassefled beasts up the easternmost of the three canyons whose confluence forms the head of the Sao Khola. At the three forks there is a line of planted willows and a grove of five small junipers, which shelter a striking black-and-yellow bird, the white-winged grosbeak. There is also a chorten and the remnants of a village, as well as a number of abandoned fields, now turned to sand, together with two high walls of caves, no longer accessible, where the lama says that he once lived as a young man.

Lama Chotuk, it appears, has always been here. He remembers the year that the great lama died, and the crops died, too, and how the monastery and the valley died together, after which his people became nomads. And his tale reflects the dearth of water in this landscape that accounts for the numbers of dead villages.

Lama Chotuk agrees to return with us to Sao Gompa and open it one last time before departing. "They are running me up and down this valley," he complains to Temba Sherpa. But he says it with the merry equanimity with which he has greeted every situation with the exception of the perished goats, and even laughs at us and clowns by sticking out a huge pink-purple tongue when asked once too often to permit a photograph. Then he is off without goodbyes, skipping nimbly down the steep gulch under the gompa. He will catch up with his yaks within the hour and vanish up the rivers to the high plateaus.

Laird and I go back downriver to the entrance of the narrow gorge near where the alleged *mehti* made its bed. Our plan is to explore the waterfalls that make this gorge impassable for horses, thinking we might descend on foot on the way out, and we discover within the first one hundred yards that for once the dire local report is true. The narrow twisting gorge with its overhanging rock, beneath which a hulking griffon has its nest in a high cave, is unrelievedly steep and broken, not by one waterfall but many, and we will be forced to climb back to the rim, traverse the plateau, and descend to the blue river once again, the way we came.

a nomad family around the yak-dung hearth

mountains between Dolpo and Mustang, as seen from the Mustang-Tibet border

OPPOSITE ~ Mount Dhaulagiri, from the nomads' high-grazing plateau near the Mustang-Tibet border

However, the reconnaissance is well worthwhile. No grazing animals have passed the tumbled boulders at the gorge's entrance, to judge from the abundance of fresh grass just beyond it. Between those boulders and the head of the first falls, a short stretch of gray torrent passed between rock beaches. On the west side, headed downstream, was one clear print of the unknown creature, and on the east side — I made my way across and followed it back upstream — a series of twelve to twenty prints headed back toward the place just above the gorge where the Lama Chotuk had shown us the *mehti*'s resting place. One might suppose — well, I suppose — that the creature ventured down toward the first falls, just as we have done, then returned back up the other side to the point where it made the tracks reported by goatherds and nomads.

This series of prints on the dark sand just above the falls are the only prints by any animal (including man) in a stretch of about thirty-five yards. Though most are now quite indistinct, they stand out readily in their progression, and at least two, which Tom Laird photographed, are as clear as the best one of the night before. Later that morning, well upstream from the originals, Laird finds another, and our measurement shows that all of them were made by the same creature — a creature of sufficient weight to make imprints that survived nearly a week in hard-packed sand.

76

Our maps indicate that this valley's elevation is about 13,000 feet. Excepting hooved animals, the only trans-Himalayan creatures large enough to make such prints are wolf and leopard, bear and man.

His Highness of Mustang-Bhot had secured what he believed to be the skin of a yeti or abominable snowman. Having some knowledge of the raja's sense of humor, I'm inclined to believe that he is having innocent fun at the expense of the credulous lowlanders, after the fashion of mountaineers the world over.

No one who travels the mountains of Nepal can avoid the yeti legend — and legend I believe it to be, for never did I encounter anyone who had actually seen the beast. Always the yeti had been seen by the great-uncle twice removed who has since moved away, or the brother of the second cousin, the one who died last year. I have been shown alleged yeti tracks, but these uneven depressions in the snow could have been made by a bear or a strayed yak.

— Toni Hagen, "Afoot in Roadless Nepal,"
National Geographic, March 1960

Similarly, Michel Peissel (in *Mustang, the Forbidden Kingdom*) dismisses the whole business as "a deliberate lie told to satisfy those 'white men' who so foolishly spent large amounts of money in search of the mythical Snowman — an invention of the sensational press of the West."

In the half century since big, upright creatures, leaving hundreds of tracks, were seen in a high snowfield on the north side of Mount Everest by a band of British mountaineers, the ye-teh, *or* yeti, *has met with a storm of disapproval from upset scientists around the world. But as with the Sasquatch of the vast rain forests of the Pacific Northwest, the case against the existence of the yeti — entirely speculation, and necessarily based on assumptions of foolishness or mendacity in many observers of good reputation — is even less "scientific" than the evidence that it exists. Photographs and casts of the yeti footprint are consistent — a very odd, broad primate foot — and so are the sight records, most of which come from the populous Sherpa country of eastern Nepal.*

*The yeti is described most often as a hairy, reddish-brown creature with a ridged crown that gives it a pointed-head appearance; in size, despite the outsized foot (entirely unlike the long foot of a bear, in which the toes are more or less symmetrical), it has been likened to an adolescent boy, though much larger individuals have been reported. There are no brown bears (*Ursos arctos*) on south side of the Himalaya, where both black bear and langur are well known and unmistakable. Bears hibernate in winter, when yetis are most often seen (in lean times, they are said to scavenge near monasteries and villages), and most yeti tracks are much too large to be made by monkeys, even in melting snow. Langurs are rarely seen in snow, or yetis either, if it comes to that: while the yeti may cross the snows on foraging excursions to higher elevations or into the next valley, its primary habitat must be the cloud forest of the myriad deep Himalayan canyons, which are exceptionally inhospitable to man. From a biologist's point of view, in fact, most of the Himalayan region is still* terra incognita. *As GS says, almost nothing is known of the natural history of the snow leopard, and we are walking a long way indeed to find out some basic information about the relatively accessible Himalayan bharal.*

One evening last month in Kathmandu, a young biologist in charge of a field project in the Arun Valley of eastern Nepal set down on our dinner table a big primate footprint in white plaster; this cast had been made in the snow outside his tent six months before. The tracks had led down across steep snowfields into valley forest; he and his colleagues were not able to follow. Plainly the creature being spoken of was the "abominable snow-

man," and I waited for GS to express skepticism. But he merely nodded, picking up the cast with care, turning it over, and setting it down again, his face frowning and intent; what interested him most, he said at last, was the similarity of this yeti print to that of the mountain gorilla. And later he told me that he was not being polite, that there was no doubt in his mind that a creature not yet scientifically described had made this print.

— The Snow Leopard [1]

(A twist of hair, which the nomads assured Laird was from a *mehti*, was submitted to George Amato, Conservation Geneticist for the Wild Life Conservation Society. He determined that the hair was from a horse. The photographs of the footprints were shown to snow leopard specialist Rodney Jackson and were later seen by Dr. George Schaller. They agreed that these prints were made by a bear — in all likelihood, the Tibetan brown bear.

Ursus arctos pruinosus is the same species as the grizzly from North America, and this *pruinosus* subspecies, George Schaller told me, is a striking creature with black legs, brown face, and a light tan back that looks "white" in certain lights and has caused this animal to be mistaken occasionally for a giant panda.

Once again the *mehti* has eluded its seekers, but there was an exciting discovery all the same. Upon seeing the tracks, I had inquired about bears, and the nomads told us that no bears were ever seen in these high desert mountains. This was borne out by the range maps I consulted at home. The Tibetan brown bear that made those prints in the Sao River Valley was the first ever recorded in Nepal. — P.M., September, 1995)

Yesterday, while I was in the gompa, Tashi, who is addicted to my binoculars, spotted a *na,* or blue sheep, crossing the high ridge of the great rock face across the river, and so today, from an old monk's cave in the canyon wall down along the valley where I go to make these notes, I scan the ridges and caragana slopes more assiduously than ever. Eventually a lammergeier makes a sudden flaring dive at something on the ridge, and there I see the sun glint on the horns of the first blue sheep I have seen since leaving Inner Dolpo twenty years ago. Soon the sheep stands, a fine big ram, and it holds this pose, all but motionless, for almost an hour, like a herald.

I spend the final afternoon on the high terrace of Sao Gompa, where the afternoon wind snaps the lonely flags and from where I can see out all across the valley. Looking upward at the clouds that fly across the rim, and the glinting sunlight on the rock, I apprehend the earth as a huge chunk of meteoric matter hurtling through the universe, now dark, now light, as it turns toward the sun the transient dew of life on its hard surface.

[1] *The Snow Leopard,* Peter Matthiessen. New York: Viking Press, 1978.

Loba on the trail, along the Kali Gandaki

Over to the east, dark clouds are forming, and in the ravine, a small flock of fire-fronted finches is taking shelter from the wind. Every afternoon has brought light snow or rain, as the monsoon pushes farther north through the Himalaya. In an hour or two this weather passes. A gray sun appears toward twilight and the evening clears, with a burning brilliance to the stars that is no longer imaginable in the smog-saturated skies of North America. When the sun vanishes behind the rim, the mountain cold falls across the canyon like an iron door, and, though it is May, we eat Pemba's good supper in down jackets.

Pemba's assistant, Sher Bahadur, scarcely speaks English, yet bringing the food, he enunciates with pleasure the name of every course and even the names of the hot water and hot milk. One cannot say enough for the wonderful spirit of these Sherpa people, who remind us day after day that no better travelling companions may be found anywhere.

Because we rise early and go hard, we are ready to lie down soon after supper, and go to sleep to the soft sound of Tashi reciting his Buddhist mantras. Out of fear of snow leopards, he now brings all the horses into camp, and all night long dozes fitfully on the ground beside them, just behind our tent. I listen with greatest contentment to their gentle stamp and blowing, which quickly dies and is replaced by the murmur of the river, flowing down across its bed of slate under the mountain.

I awaken to a brief sweet birdsong that may be the blue-headed redstart observed yesterday. At daybreak, emerging from the tent, I am stirred to see the untethered and unfenced animals standing so patiently beside their guardian, who permitted himself real sleep toward first light.

Mount Dhaulagiri at sunset

Within the walls of the city, the large white cube is the palace and the red ones are Chyodi, Champa, and Tugchen temples. The view here is from the south.

◩ Lo Monthang

After a fortnight in northeastern Lo, we return to the headwaters of the Kali Gandaki, making our way along the river and climbing at last to the valleys and plateaus of western Lo, which by comparison to the east, are densely populated (there are only about six thousand Loba in the entire kingdom). The largest settlement is Lo Monthang, a small fort-city on a tableland at 12,400 feet between two ravines that descend to the main river. (Lo derives from *"Lho,"* south borderland of Tibet, or *"Glo bo,"* the region's name in the earliest 7th century Tibetan chronicles. *Smon thanq* — on most maps "Mustang" — has been translated "Fertile Plain of Medicinal Herbs.") This narrow plain between snow ranges, which exceed 20,000 feet to the west, is the northernmost and largest in all Lo.

With its twenty-foot-high surrounding wall and its sentinel turrets at each corner, with its prayer flags and white central palace and red temples, Lo Monthang seems formidable and enormous by comparison to the other isolated settlements we have passed through, yet this medieval town on its remote desert plateau is thought to have but one hundred and eighty households, and less than one thousand inhabitants, and one could circumambulate the city walls four times in an hour, as King Jigme Palbar Bista, on his royal constitutional, is said to do at sunrise every morning. [➡ 93]

Lo Monthang, from the north

FOLLOWING PAGES ~ *palace and the red Chyodi Monastery*

❖ 87 ❖

the roofs of Lo Monthang, outlined with precious wood

BELOW ~ *Tashi Chusang's painted map of Lo Monthang shows the relative importance, for Loba, of the temples, palace and houses. The red buildings (left to right) are the Tugchen, Champa, and Chyodi temples; the white building is the palace.*

In the foreground is one corner turret of the walled city, and at the far end stands the opposite turreted corner — this is the longest diagonal across the city.

Chortens await the weary pilgrim at each corner of the city, whose fortified gate is in a cul-de-sac in the northeast corner, protected from the Himalayan winds that in the afternoon may mount vast desert dust storms from the south. The gate stands behind large pink entrance chortens and prayer walls of inscribed stones. The white palace rises just inside the gate, and the red temples and monastery are west of the palace, in a north-south line that is almost the length of the fort. Small houses reached by winding cobbled alleys fill most of the remaining space, and most (including the one where we are staying) are built against the outside walls, with access from their flat roofs to the walkway that runs all around the parapets. Outside the wall at the south end is an enclosure containing two huge sacred cottonwoods in which the dark kites that drift over the city have their shaggy nest.

Prayer flags fly everywhere on the roofs of Lo Monthang, and each roof is stacked along its edge with brushwood, used to kindle cooking fires in the mud stoves (the fuel at this high altitude is dried dung), and it has been interesting to note the change in the character of this wood as we moved northward. In Jomsom, which lies close to the fir forests, there are woodpiles of small logs, in Tange small limbs, whereas here in this high desert it is meager thornbush, scoured from the stony mountainsides above. Poplar and willow saplings are nursed in small stone-walled enclosures near the towns, but like the new limbs on the cropped cottonwoods, they are much too precious to be used as fuel and are saved for construction purposes, mostly ceilings and roof beams.

Lo's culture and language are mostly derived from Tibet, and its subsistence economy is largely based on trade in agricultural and animal products. Barley and buckwheat, cultivated by methods at least ten centuries old, are the grains that fare best at these altitudes, where a short growing season and a chronic shortage of good soil, water, and fertilizer severely limit growth. Like most of the towns above 10,000 feet, Lo Monthang is limited to one crop each year — the one favored here is mixed wheat and peas — with a few mustard greens. Bread and farina, with a little hard cheese and endless cups of butter tea, are the foundation of the high Himalayan diet, but meat and fat are eaten, too, mostly mutton stew.　　　　　　[➡ 98]

Dhungmara Himal and Rani's Fort; the chortens of one hundred thousand blessings dominate one corner of the walled city.

Children, women, and men work furiously to harvest wheat during September.

bringing in the sheaves, Gemi village

a woman's sharp sickle, kept near to hand

Here in the Himalayan rain shadow — and the dry abandoned fields all around bear witness to the lack of water — there is little snow or rain, only the dessicating winds and burning sunshine, the bare sky. Except in the irrigated places, the landscapes all around the town are pale and sere as any desert, the natural and increasing drought made worse by centuries of over-cutting, overgrazing, over-intensive use of the poor soil. The inevitable erosion of a fragile land-scape is compounded by the replacement of scarce wood fuel by animal dung that would have helped to nourish and stabilize the fields, and perhaps man has played a greater role than has been thought in the abandonment to desert of palace-forts and villages up and down the river. Two centuries ago, by all accounts, parts of this country were still forested. Today almost all the wood used in construction is carried north on the backs of animals from the Hi-malayan forests.

On a pale dune high above the city to the north stands the ruin of the old palace-fort of Kechar Dzong, with the bones of ancient settle-ment and terraces spread out below it, disappearing under desert sand. One morning I rode up there with Tashi and Ang Temba, trav-elling around the head of the north ravine by way of the red-and-gray-striped Nyamgal Monastery, built originally in the same period as Lo Monthang and rebuilt a few years ago after a fire. Nyamgal is a monastery of Sakya, the main Buddhist sect of Lo (and also of Mon-golia). We make an offering of butter lamps and keep on going, scat-tering sand-colored lizards as the horses climb the sand ridge to the small ruin of the Rani's Fort (Rani Dzong) and higher still to Kechar Dzong, from where, biting the wind, we have a splendid view north, east, and west over Tibet as well as a southward prospect down over the ridges and valleys of western Lo to Annapurna.

To the north the broad sinuous trail of the old trading route dis-appears over the brown ridge into Tibet, and one can see cliffs of the valley's central ridge where, centuries ago, the headwaters of the Kali Gandaki burst a new channel north of Kechar Dzong, deflecting the source of its irrigation system and dooming the fort-city and the fields beneath.

It is supposed that this greatest calamity in Lo's history occurred just prior to A.D. 1420, when Ama-dpal, or Amepal, ruler of the fort-cities of the Kali Gandaki and first king of the modern lineage — one *molla* (or "record of ancient rhetoric") calls him "famous as the sun and moon" — made his legendary descent from Kechar Dzong to found Lo Monthang on the south side of the ravine. Under Amadpal, a revered Tibetan lama named Ngorchen Kunga Dzangpo led the construction of most of Lo's great monasteries and temple buildings.

winnowing buckwheat, at Trenkar, with Dhungmara Himal in the background

To the east of that rupture in the ridge is the red canyon leading to Chosar village, where in recent years, another cataclysm destroyed the fields, in the same great flood that scoured the immense gorge through which we rode north in mid-May. High in the mountains to the west is the sacred glacier that provides water to Lo Monthang and the low-caste settlement in the ravine between the city and Kechar Dzong, and in afternoon light one can see thin silver glitterings of the stream descending the dark mountain. The Loba, who fear their remorseless shrinking glacier, know nothing about global warming or other manmade pollutions that seem certain to bring their ancient culture to an end. [➡ III]

harvesting wheat, Lo Monthang

threshing wheat, Gemi village

Across the ravine from Gemi's active fields, abandoned farmland speaks loudly of the desertification of Mustang. More fields have been abandoned for lack of irrigation water — due to shrinking glaciers — than those currently under cultivation.

A gleaner picks up individual heads of stray wheat, accidentally left in the fields during harvest. Farmers work six months in fields that often produce only enough to feed their families eight months out of the year.

FOLLOWING PAGES ~ *The raja, on royal wheat harvest day, oversees the villagers who have come to harvest his wheat. Traditionally, every household in Lo Monthang sends one person to harvest the raja's wheat, and no one else's fields may be harvested until his are finished.*

peas drop from the chaff as this woman winnows

*The Loba winnow their wheat crop outside the walls of
Lo Monthang. When the wind dies down, the winnowers
stand in place calling the wind: "ku, ku, ku."*

◈ "LIKE A HIDDEN VALLEY"

TASHI TENZING, THE HEAD LAMA OF LO, IS A HANDSOME SOFT-VOICED silver-haired man who sits in the cold spring sun on an upper terrace of Chyodi Monastery, pasting skull faces onto his papier-mâché demon masks for the Tiji Festival of masked lama dancing that begins tomorrow. Chyodi is the last large training monastery in Lo, since Champa Lha-kang and Tugchen Lha-kang, with their great art treasures, are now no more than sacred shrines or temples.

We present the traditional white silk *kata* scarves which he returns in blessing, draping them around our necks. Then Tom Laird offers him a photograph of the beautiful Maitreya Buddha figure in the Champa temple, and he touches it reverently to his forehead. Ri-Dorje, the big fierce-looking young monk who had come to fetch us at the house by the town wall and escort us past the monastery's free-ranging mastiffs (trained to attack anyone not dressed in maroon), brings cushions and butter tea as Lama Tashi continues cutting cardboard and a hoopoe makes its dove-like call from somewhere in the city. Periodically the monk urges butter tea upon the lama — for great lamas, like kings, are not to show interest in such mundane things — and when the lama excuses himself to visit the toilet chamber on the roof, Ri-Dorje offers a respectful bow in that direction.

The Kingdom of Lo is referred to in a 7th-century Tibetan history called *The Blue Annals,* and its culture had continued for a thousand years before Nepal came into existence. Tashi Tenzing says that the kings of ancient Lo were rulers of all of West Tibet and as far south as Muktinath in Nepal, and that Lo Monthang was formerly an urban center that dominated the great trade route of the Kali Gandaki, attracting numbers of artists, scholars, and pilgrims, making its own pottery and casting its own metal, including many of the superb Buddha figures that are still to be seen in the decaying monasteries. That is why its early monasteries were so huge — the Dharma halls and altars of Champa and Tugchen are comparable to all but the largest in Tibet.

Lo's decline began after its greatest era between A.D. 1400 and 1600, due to constant warfare between the feudal states of Ngari or West Tibet but also, perhaps, due to exhaustion of the dry environment. Today, as scholar David Jackson remarks, Lo is "one of the most remote, backward, and inaccessible valleys in the Nepal Himalaya."

Tashi Tenzing, abbot of Chyodi Monastery, Lo Monthang

In his own gentle, humorous, and profound way, Lama Tashi is as natural and free as Lama Chotuk, the wild quick Kagyu lama at Sao Khola. He is acquainted with that nomad lama — "he is a good man, a little bald, like me" — and he also knows a lot about the *shrungma* deities in that black chapel at Sao Gompa. Long ago, it was a Sakya monastery, and so the oldest paintings there are Sakya, but those *shrungma* deities, he says, are Kagyu, especially Mahakala, the big blue figure at the center of the group, and Cha-me, the fearsome red guardian in Tatar chain mail out of Central Asia. Sadly he confirms the Khamba thefts, which included twenty to thirty superb *tankas* or painted cloth scrolls, and many fine statues fashioned here in Lo.

Though he supposes it was built a little later than Champa (1420), or about 1480, the lama does not know the real age of Sao Gompa. "There used to be many people there, living in cave villages as well as houses, so they built the gompa. In those days, there were many fields and trees." Here he paused to draw a map of Sao Khola's landmarks and habitations, including the river confluence and two sacred springs, saying that he himself had travelled up all three rivers. "There were many fields and houses up that river to the east, and many trees up the river to the west."

After a pause, he said, "That place is like a *bayul* — like what we know as 'a hidden valley.'"

"In Lo we have no trees to speak of but they had plenty there. They even had rice, while we have trouble growing wheat! It was a place of plenty, and so we say it was like a "hidden valley," to be opened only as a refuge for the righteous in periods of world destruction." Still snipping cardboard, the lama was speaking with great care, as if cutting out each word with his ancient shears. "Or if in a previous life one had great merit, one might be reborn into that peaceful place, without trouble or strife — but still a human world, where people are wise enough to pay very close attention to the Dharma."

The *bayul* or hidden valley — Shambhala is an example — is a kind of paradise on earth but also a complex metaphysical idea. Suffice it to say that it is dangerous and difficult to reach and elusive even when one gets there, and that Laird and I had already had peculiar intuitions of this kind about Sao Khola. But the lama had been at pains to say, "*Like* a hidden valley," and though in esoteric Buddhist teachings it is customary to phrase things indirectly, to avoid contaminating the immediacy of the-thing-itself, he was also indicating that Sao Khola was not truly a *bayul,* not any longer.

Tashi Tenzing's dorje *and* tilbu *in their carrying case — the lama takes them on his travels throughout Mustang to officiate at rituals.*

Tashi Tenzing leads a fire-offering ceremony (using his dorje *and* tilbu*), started on a sand mandala, in the home of the Pasang Lama (seated left). This ceremony of initiation and empowerment took place two months before Tiji as part of Pasang's preparation to be the chief dancer in that ceremony.*

"Here is the legend. Sao Gompa had a lama of the highest spiritual attainment. In a ceremony to renew fertility, he put a few rice grains in a pot, telling his attendant not to take the lid off until rice filled the pot to overflowing. Then he went off up the river and disappeared behind the peak. Seeing vultures gather at that place, the attendant was sure that his master had perished when in fact he was offering teachings to the vultures. Thus he felt free to disregard instructions and lifted the lid from the boiling pot just as the rice was coming to the top. As a result, the fields stopped producing rice. Though wheat grew for a few years, the water from the *himal* dried up so that even growing wheat became impossible. The people abandoned the valley and became nomads." Lama Tashi talked as if the people's return to the nomad life had occurred long, long ago, whereas Lama Chotuk had referred to it as if it had taken place in his own lifetime — not necessarily a contradiction from a Buddhist point of view — adding that his father had tried to reestablish the old gardens and had failed.

Tashi Tenzing approved of our intention to disguise the name and whereabouts of "Sao Gompa," since people could break in and steal the treasures that are still left. "The local people are afraid of those deities up there, knowing that anyone who stole the temple

Pasang's family tends the hearth fire in order to supply tea and food to Tashi Tenzing and Pasang during the ceremony.

treasures would die within two or three years. But people don't live there anymore because it's such a powerful place, and the custodian only goes every ten days or so to light a butter lamp, so it's not good if a lot of people find it. "If people go," he said, "the *mehti* are going to leave."

Lama Tashi did not seem in the least surprised that we had seen those tracks. "There is a *mehti* at Sao Khola," he said, calmly and carefully. "Since I was young, we have always heard reports of footprints and hair and even sightings in that region." The nomads have told Lama Tashi that the creature comes to remote villages and that once when the Lama was performing a ceremony at one of these villages, a boy disappeared, then showed up again, saying he'd seen it. "I didn't see it there," he added, snipping away at cardboard for the masks, "but I saw it in Kham [eastern Tibet] when I was 26. That was 1950 — I am 68 this year." He saw footprints only last summer in the nomad land, at and said that a few years ago, there were lots of footprints found. The people never saw them but there were prints all over where they were digging out *peh-musa,* the long-tailed marmot. *Mehti*s are plentiful in the border region, he told us, glad that Laird had obtained pictures of the tracks.

"Three or four years ago, I went to China [though they recognize Tibet as a separate entity, the people of Lo, after thirty years, accept the reality that Tibet has become part of China]. A neighbor boy near the house where I was staying in the village of Lak Shan went out to graze his animals and saw a *mehti*. The child was startled and began yelling, and threw stones at the *mehti*, and the *mehti* got mad and smashed the boy against the rocks and killed him. The farmer attacked the *mehti* with a knife and stabbed it in the side, and the *mehti* bled and yelled like a man, but it killed the farmer. So I was told — I did not see the bodies."

While the lama drew a map of these alleged *mehti* episodes and sightings, Monk Ri-Dorje offered us *sham-dur* and lollipops. *Sham-dur* is raw sheep meat ground to powder, then mixed with chili peppers as a cold soup, and it was without exception the best thing I would taste the entire time I was in Lo.

"The number of *mehti*s went way down between 1960 and 1974, when so many armed Khampas were back there in the mountains. Now that they are gone, the reports of *mehti* are increasing once again. It appears that the Chinese, riding their vehicles on patrol along the border shooting off their guns, may have driven more *mehti* into the Sao Khola region. I can't say how many there might be, but I am told they reproduce like dogs, with three to four young every year. They are hairy, too, like dogs, with their hind end a little up in the air, a little long." (This sounded suspiciously like a langur, though no langur made those tracks.) "Mostly they walk on all fours, but when they walk upright, they hold their hands up" — here he made the strange gesture, demonstrated earlier by our horse man Bishnaduki, with the arms held high and out in front and the hands flopped down about the level of the ears.

"Our people don't think of them as spirits, deities. People are afraid of them, especially when they are with young. If you leave them alone, they won't bother you, but if you surprise one along the trail, it might bite you and even kill you. Bears will bite, too, but at least they won't attack you with hurled rocks!" Amusing himself, the lama was warming to his subject, still working carefully on his map, but I had no feeling he was laughing at us. "No, the *mehti* is not a deity, it is an animal. Where there are no caves, it lives in holes that it burrows in the ground. In winter, it sleeps for a month or two, just like a bear. It has an unusual physical strength, and a *sems* or *mun* [a conscious spirit-energy] like man, and hands like man. Dogs don't have *sems* but men and *mehti*s do. There are many kinds of beings. The most dangerous ones are demons, then monkeys, then *mehti*s, then human beings — these four are a similar class of being, with the same *mun* or *sems*."

Here during the Tiji Ceremony, Tashi Tenzing is besieged by children and adults who are anxious to have his blessing.

Everything the lama said seemed to justify the excitement we had felt in the Sao Khola. Glaring at me, Laird was clutching the lama's map in a proprietary way, for he had been grievously afflicted by the *mehti* fever that has struck down many a Himalayan traveller before him, myself included. Though he later thought better of it, he muttered in English that he would not share this map with me, after which he asked the lama about his chances of seeing a *mehti*, were he to spend some time this summer with the nomads.

"I'm not going to predict you will because you might blame me if you don't," the lama said, "but if you spend time with the nomads, there is a good chance you might see one." [⟼ 126]

Bell in hand, Tashi Tenzing blesses a monk inside Chyodi Monastery.

Tashi Tenzing blesses two women in his small private quarters.

Tashi Chusang, herbalist, painter, royal astrologer, and maker of charms, is the other ritual specialist in Lo Monthang. He is married, and his home is his atelier and medical clinic. Tashi Tenzing is celibate and lives in the monastery. Both men serve the raja and the community as ritual specialists and elders.

For many rituals, string spirit catchers, such as the one he is making and the one in the offering, are required.

Charms such as this one made from a sheep's skull, with faded spirit catcher in the center, are mounted over the doors of many households in Mustang, and are said to keep ghosts and witches out of the house. OPPOSITE ~ *printed charm pasted to a front door*

Tashi Chusang pauses from his painting to prepare an herbal compound for a patient.

Tashi Chusang and his son prepare herbs for medicine.

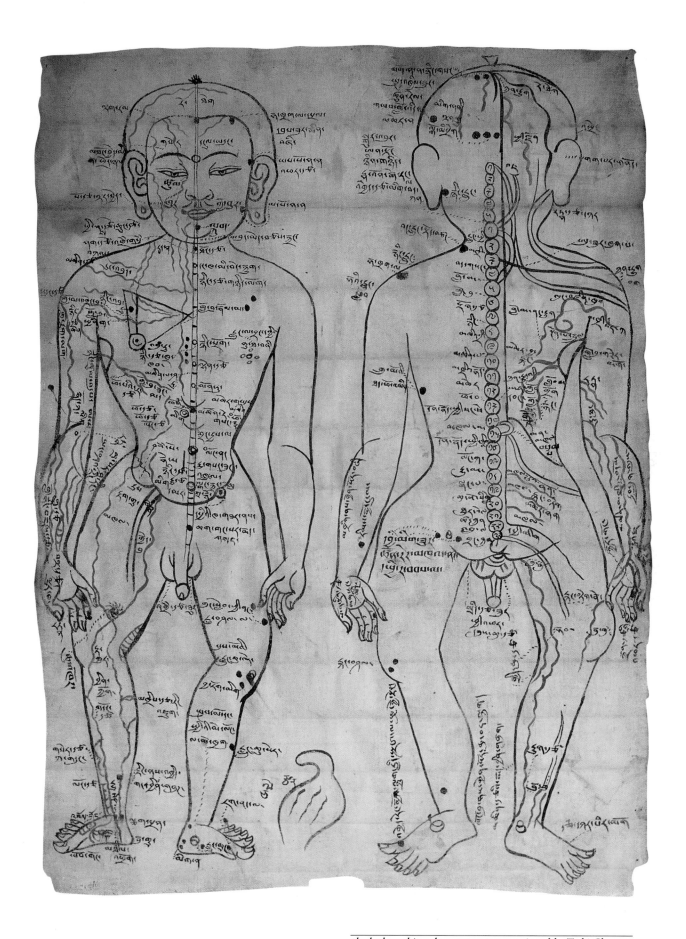

the body and its relevant structures as viewed by Tashi Chusang

125

⊞ R A J A J I G M E

The raja of Lo was just returned from a journey to Tibet, where he had accompanied a group of Loba anxious to set up trade. Beyond the border they had encountered two soldiers who had seen a *mehti* that same day but had not shot at it, for fear that the wounded creature might attack and kill them. The raja and his group went straight to the scene, where all twelve had a good look at the fresh *mehti* tracks. Sitting on a beautiful red carpet in his reception room, the raja lifted a small booted foot. "It was about the same size as this shoe," he told us.

Raja Jigme seemed disturbed by our journey to Sao Gompa, of which he remarked cryptically, as if in warning, "There are very powerful deities in that valley." Fearing theft of the remaining statues, he decided that in the future, nobody would be permitted to go there.

Last fall, as the only foreigner in Lo, Tom Laird was befriended by the raja, who gave him a Lhasa apso puppy as well as the run of the royal palace. Raja Jigme Parwar Bista is a friendly moon-faced man with a fine rich laugh, though his eyes are withdrawn and rather private. A big man in his early sixties, he is an expert horseman, proud of his horses, and manages a team of five in threshing his own wheat fields in the autumn. His wife, who is called Rani Sahib, is a pale high-caste Tibetan (by tradition, all the queens of Lo come from Tibet), very elegant and beautiful, with two prominent gold teeth in the left side of her upper jaw. She has the sad eyes of a sybil and a strong nose that makes her profile beautiful in a very different and unexpected way, as if one were looking at two heads in one.

The raja and rani of Mustang, dressed for King Birendra's coronation in Kathmandu in 1975.

The rani of Mustang with her ladies, Tsering Yuten and Dawa. The raja of Mustang with the mayor of Lo Monthang, Pema Ongdi, and a group of nobles. The raja and rani dress in official robes and jewelry for festivals and weddings — in this case, for Tiji.

Some years ago, this royal couple lost their only child, a boy of eight, and the rani has borne no other children, but the raja will not take another wife to produce an heir. This is a serious matter, since he himself is regarded as the twenty-fifth in the straight line of descent from Ama-dpal. "I brought her so far from her home," he once told Laird, "and she would hurt so." Eventually the crown will pass to his brother's son, the Crown Prince Jigme Singi Palbar Bista, who lives in Kathmandu but has come here for the Tiji Festival. With the crown prince are four Europeans — business associates, it appears. (The crown prince is said to have interests in the Tibetan rug industry — New Zealand wool, European capital, peasant weavers — that has replaced tourism as Nepal's foremost industry and is rapidly despoiling the fragile ecology of the Kathmandu Valley.) These four, with three French photographers and a Japanese TV crew, all of them arrived today, are the only foreigners in Lo Monthang besides myself and Laird, who believes we will be the first outsiders ever to witness the legendary masked lama dances. [➡ 138]

Raja Jigme threshes his pea crop with a team of four horses. "Horses, like the land, can be of use to us for many years if we don't drive them too hard. . . . We work nearly as hard as they do, so we understand at once if a horse is hurting or tired or being driven too fast."

Raja Jigme is very religious and performs this special ritual — meditation for the Kings of The Four Directions — every day. For the Loba, the purity of the raja and all his actions, ritual and otherwise, is reflected in the purity of their land. Any fault in his religious practice could disturb the harmony between men and gods.

TOP ~ *Though Nepalese adjudication is available — three days' walk away — Loba still prefer to have the raja judge their disputes about water rights, inheritance, and petty crime. Capital crimes are tried in Jomsom.* BOTTOM ~ *The raja presides over a town meeting in the ruined lower story of the Champa Lha-khang — a temple founded by the raja's grandfather 23 times removed.*

TOP ~ *A peasant of Trenkar approaches the raja in the middle of the harvest with a request that he solve a dispute about the alleged maiming of a horse.* BOTTOM ~ *A royal servant serves the raja a cup of tea while he mediates a grazing rights dispute.*

A monk prints prayer flags in the palace.

BELOW ~ *The raja helps the monks string prayer flags from the palace roof. Such rituals gain merit for the household and, in this case, for all subjects of the raja.*

OPPOSITE ~ *The rani pours fresh water into silver offering bowls on her private altar.*

This image of Phagpa Lokesvara was probably modeled on a much smaller original in the Potala Palace, Lhasa. It is housed in the Golden Chapel inside the raja's fort in Charang. This manifestation of Lokesvara was the tutelary deity of King Songsten Gampo who unified Tibet in the 7th century. Its presence in a royal chapel in Mustang indicates the strong religious and social links that the nobility of Lo had with Tibet.

The rajas of Mustang have always been patrons of the Dharma. In about 1425 the first great raja of Lo, Amepal, founded the walled city of Lo Monthang. At the same time he ordered the painting of the murals in the Champa Temple, and commissioned a silver- and gold-covered edition of the Buddhist scriptures. Originally there were one hundred and eight volumes — each with a cover as finely worked as the one here, which is preserved in the raja's private chapel in his palace in Lo Monthang; the others have vanished. Over the centuries, many other Buddhist texts, all embellished with fine paintings and calligraphy, were created for the temples of Lo.

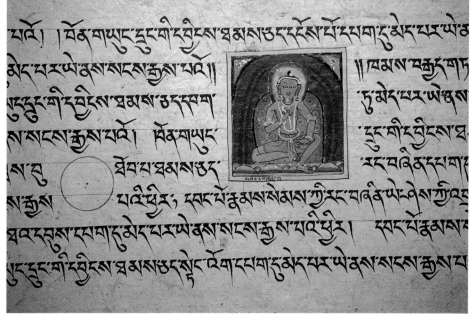

◈ THE TIJI CEREMONY

THE TIJI CEREMONY BEGAN ON THE 29TH OF MAY IN THE MAIN square east of the palace, under snappeting prayer flags, white cracked walls, and blue-framed windows. On the second-floor balcony of the palace, glowering down upon the celebrants, is a huge old mastiff, traditionally accoutred in red ruff (another mastiff, this one stuffed, hangs like a mobile from the ceiling on the second landing, in ceaseless vigil against demons).

Early in the afternoon, horns resounded — the short horn or *kagyling,* which announces the two twelve-foot copper *dunchens,* with their elephantine blartings, followed by two double-reeded

A former royal guard dog (a rare red mastiff) guards the entrance to the palace even in death.

horns (the player is trained to blow with a peculiar technique of double-breathing), all accompanied by drum and cymbals. The striking gold-green-red-blue spiral painted in the center of the drum represents "the ceaseless becoming of Mind," an ancient symbol also reflected in the saligram.

Next, an ancient and enormous *tanka* three stories high was unrolled down the entire south wall of the square. The *tanka* portrayed Padma Sambhava (or "Guru Rinpoche") who brought this ceremony to Tibet in the 8th century (it is said to have originated in Afghanistan) and founded the Nyingma sect of Tibetan Buddhism. Following an incense purification, the healer-lama and religious painter Tashi Chusang, accompanied by Crown Prince Jigme in black fur hat, black leather boots, and tailored traditional dress, made an offering of six brass bowls of grain, set out on a wood altar with the painted cakes made from butter and farina that we had seen fashioned the day before by a group of monks in a chapel of the palace.

one of two giant appliqué tankas *displayed during the Tiji Ceremony*

At midafternoon, in high wind and blowing dust, eleven lamas in maroon and gold, wearing high red hats, came from the palace and took their places along the wall beneath the *tanka,* with Tashi Tenzing on the elevated seat just in the center. At one end of the line, big Ri-Dorje and an older monk commence a sonorous overture on the twelve-foot horns, which are supported at the open end by a carved wood stand. Horns and drums are accompanied by cymbals struck more or less casually by all the lamas except Tashi Tenzing, who in his gentle, inobtrusive way appears to do *everything* with complete attention, and not only attention but quiet celebration of every moment of his life.

As the monks and lamas commence chanting, twelve more monks come from the palace in maroon and royal blue and glittering gold brocade, with cymbal-shaped hats decked with upright peacock plumes. Soon they withdraw, to be replaced by the masked dancers who introduce the Tiji myth, explained to us yesterday by Tashi Tenzing in the course of a second visit to Chyodi.

The myth is a long one, taking three days to enact, but briefly it concerns a deity named Dorje Jono, who is fated to save his people from the scourge of his own father, a terrible demon who has wreaked havoc on the land, bringing about a shortage of the precious water, causing their animals to miscarry, and creating all manner of disasters that threaten a dearth of water, famine, and an end to their society. (A dearth of water is the greatest ill that can possibly befall this culture, and has already befallen it, in that centuries-old shift of the great Kali Gandaki that caused the abandonment of the original fort-castle of Kechar Dzong.) Dorje Jono repels the demon through the power of his magical dancing — he dances fifty-two separate dances, one of them in ten different bodies, each with a different head — in the course of which he finds time to poke fun at the clownish figures of a Hindu yogin and a Chinese Chan (Zen) master. As the dances end, Dorje Jono kills the demon, after which his people are relieved of their plague of misfortunes, water becomes plentiful once more, and the balance and harmony of existence are restored. Thus Tiji (from *ten che — the hope of Buddha Dharma prevailing in all worlds* — "not just Lo," Lama Tashi says, "but Germany! Everywhere!") is effectively a spring renewal festival, an enactment of the culture myth that is based, like all else, on precious water, the source of which is now confined to that small, shrinking glacier in the western peaks.

Tashi Tenzing and other senior monks sit underneath a tanka, *on the first day of Tiji, as the first dance commences.*

Raja Jigme, who adjudicates his people's problems, says that all they ever talk about are water and horses. Recently a woman was fined five hundred rupees (about ten dollars, a very large sum by local standards) for carelessly misdirecting one of the small irrigation channels, which are controlled by small mud dams opened and closed by hand. The five hundred rupees were distributed to the people whose fields had been deprived.

▣ CHAMPA TEMPLE

BECAUSE EACH DAY OF TIJI SEEMS TO START IN THE AFTERNOON, WE are free to make excursions in the morning. One day we visited the great red Champa Lha-kang, a temple dedicated to Maitreya, the future Buddha, whose enormous clay figure behind the altar soars toward the beamed ceiling and disappears downward into the darkness of a closed floor below. The Buddha figure, six hundred years old, is surrounded by superb round paintings — the world's greatest surviving collection of 15th-century mandalas, says Tom Laird.

Champa's upper wall is supported by wood columns perhaps eighteen inches in diameter, or very much larger than any tree now to be found in parched Mustang. The columns are constructed out of sections like big upright logs, and one imagines them, one to a side, on the dusty swaying backs of yaks, toiling and blowing up the Kali Gandaki from the forests of India. All around the altar room are magnificent frescoes, and the mandala on the rear wall to the left of the great Buddha figure is, in Laird's opinion, a true masterpiece of line and detail, color and floral patterns. On this one he discovered a signed inscription — *I have come from Kathmandu to paint this picture* — and he now believes that most or all of the other mandalas, which are fine indeed but not of this luminous quality, were done by disciples under this man's supervision. The mandalas represent many years of painstaking work in what must have been near darkness, and went largely unseen for century after century until the scholar Giuseppe Tucci arrived here in the early 1950s. Dr. Tucci predicted that these wonderful old temples, Champa and Tugchen, would scarcely survive his own departure, and it is true that they cry out for repair lest they go the way of a third temple called Samdruling, a few miles to the southwest, which was still standing as late as 1963. After that date, Lo was closed to foreigners for thirty years, and today Samdruling is gone.

Large crowds gather in the square in front of the palace to watch the Tiji
Ceremony; the masked deity in the center of the circle is Dorje Jono.

At the huge windowless Tugchen Lha-kang, the altar room is one hundred fifteen feet long by sixty five feet wide and thirty feet high, or as large as those in all but a few Tibetan temples. Like Champa, it has an ancient *aka* floor — not hard clay as in other buildings but a kind of worked pebble cement. Its columns are square instead of round, and a row of sharp-toothed wooden lions circles the central light well. (These lions also preside over the Jo-khang temple in Lhasa, the most celebrated building in the Tibetan capital besides the Potala Palace of the Dalai Lamas.) Though the walls are of mud brick, five feet thick in places, the wooden doors and columns, as well as Champa's giant Maitreya Buddha, convey the massive strength of the great wood Buddhist temples that were built in India in early times and are found to this day in Japan.

For the second day of Tiji, numbers of Loba have arrived from the outlying hamlets, and the small square is thronged with wild beautiful people, with all of the women and children, at least, in traditional dress. The crowd is cheerful and unnaturally clean, though plenty of dirty ones turn up to maintain old standards, and a few, drunk on *chang*, are sprawled in the small wood doorways. On the south wall the great ancient *tanka* has been replaced by another no less than a century old, Laird thinks, a tapestry of fine silk brocade, embroidered in Tibet in the last days of the old regime and brought by the raja's father from Lhasa.

Again today, the ceremonies do not start until early afternoon, by which time the great wind out of India has catapulted a huge dust storm onto the plain. No doubt the tardiness accommodates the newcomers, some of whom, including Lama Pema Nu from Yara, have travelled a considerable distance. I spent the first part of the day far up the mountainside, tracing the braided irrigation runnels back up through the willow plots and stone-walled fields to the clear brook that comes down off the glacier. (Before serfdom was abolished by a decree of the Nepal Congress in 1956, the raja of Lo owned most of the land and the people, too, and could have any peasant removed at will. Even today, some villages are expected to supply labor for the raja's fields.) By the time I descend the mountainside to Lo Monthang, and join the madding crowd in the palace square, the dark winds and monsoon clouds I have fled for the last hour are upon us. However, the crowd is not dismayed by the dust whipped into its round faces and joyfully laughs and whistles at the antics of the clowns, who are two diminutive masked monks less than ten years old. With the bright masks and many-colored costumes, the hard mountain light, the log-laddered earthen dwellings with their flat roofs crowded by strong brown black-braided Asiatic faces, the scene is eerily reminiscent of the kachina dances of the Hopi and Pueblo peoples of the American Southwest, where in recent years, Hopi spiritual leaders and Tibetan lamas have been discussing all sorts of ancient correspondences between their peoples.

Dolpo pilgrims — with human thigh-bone horn and a ritual drum — come to to see the famous temples of Lo Monthang.

Eventually the raja appears in turquoise-green wool boots and regal purple robe, and Rani Sahib, also in purple, wears a whole crown of tiny river pearls set off by dozens of large red coralline stones interspersed with matched ornaments of turquoise. The crown prince, too, wears purple, as well as a shirt of fire-gold over neat Western trousers and black leather boots. All are attended by royal relatives and nobles, the men in peaked hats of gold brocade, the women in imperial displays of turquoise and silver.

Trailing after the royal party are the German and Norwegian businessmen, decked out in parodies of local dress, gold hats perched high on their long Western heads (the embarrassed young woman in the party had sense enough to dispense with the funny hats). At one point the raja's sister is moved out of her chair and the German moved into it so that he may appear on Japanese TV with the royal party. All of these odd figures, between masked dances, present themselves before Lama Tashi Tenzing, who drapes each craned neck with a white silk *kata* or red ribbon. Even the TV crew, whose camera and sound boom wrapped in gleaming plastic against the dust, has been obtrusive in the ceremony since its three-thousand-dollar per hour helicopter shattered the sun and mountain silences on the first morning. The members are given *katas* by the lama, and are thoroughly photographed by one another in the process.

145

It would be easier to deplore the eager Westerners and hustling Japanese (seeking to give permanence to this ancient celebration of renewal — hence impermanence), were we not among the auslanders ourselves. Fortunately we outsiders are very few, all but lost in the horde of undefended merry faces. The costumes and masks, the twelve-foot horns, the gold cups of wheat, the butter cakes, the snow peaks and wind and dust and sun, the *mehti*, snow leopard, snow pigeons, saligrams, the dying glacier and the desert ruins, the drunks and rajas and foreigners, the dogs and yaks. Tantra!

During Tiji, old social ties are renewed and business is not forgotten. Lakpah Tsering (right), a servant of the raja's, shows — for the curious eyes of Pema Tenzing (left) and his family — a piece of turquoise he acquired while in Tibet with the raja.

THE TEMPLES OF LO MONTHANG

THIS MORNING WE RETURNED TO CHAMPA FOR ANOTHER LOOK AT the wonderful mandalas, and while we were there, measured the room and the Maitreya figure, fifty feet tall, which until a few years ago was the largest Buddha figure in Nepal. I lit five butter lamps to the future Buddha and made my alien bows and said goodbye.

From Champa we proceeded to the palace, where the raja was holding informal court for visiting dignitaries and lamas. He was seated in front of the west window, silhouetted by the bright reflections from the snow peaks behind. Among the twenty or thirty men drinking butter tea along the walls were our friend Lama Pema Nu of Yara and our affable hostler-hustler Bishnaduki, who is a minor courtier of noble family and a wearer of the golden hat in the Tiji Ceremony. As in medieval courts, the assemblage was serenaded by a *damyin*, or Tibetan guitar, to which a rickety old man began to dance and sing, smiling as crazily as a court jester. Then a solemn young boy took over on the *damyin*, and two men danced, seriously now, and the boy danced, too, even as he played. The old Loba song they sang honors the raja: "On the golden ridge we raise the golden flag . . ." These court musicians come from the outcast blacksmith caste that lives outside the city. They neither eat nor drink from plates or glasses used by other Loba.

On the way out, the raja invites Laird and me to come here to the palace for the midday meal, which is presided over by Rani Sahib. We dine on an excellent rice-and-onion dish with pickled radishes, noodles with three different species of wild mushrooms, potatoes, and mustard greens. Among those present is Tsewang, the raja's nephew, who describes again the *mehti* prints he had seen with his uncle and the royal party in Tibet.

Outside the room, the courtiers prepare two ancient Tibetan muskets — blunderbusses, really, since the muzzles are flared wide like horns — to be used to finish off the demon in this afternoon's grand finale to the Tiji Ceremony. The muskets are rigged with two bayonet-like spikes that swing down from the muzzle to support the front end (the nomads use paired antelope horns), to increase the chances of striking the infernal target.

Toward the end of yesterday's ceremonies, after the royal party had departed, the masked dancers, clad in animal masks — mastiff, raven, snow leopard, red deer, and other beasts less easily identified — joined forces to attack the demon, who had been reduced by all the rites to a cloth doll perhaps two feet long. Into this figure was thrust in an interminable ceremony a series of blue daggers, until just at dark, the demon's pitiful remains were borne away into the palace, and the line of cold wind-swept lamas under the huge *tanka* became free to leave. Departing the courtyard, Lama Tashi Tenzing, still attentive and still smiling, touched the foreheads of the little children who ran forward to be blessed, even while the great *tanka* was pulled away from the wall so that all present would walk beneath and touch their heads to it and receive the Guru Rinpoche's universal blessing.

◈ THE DEMON'S RED REMNANTS

ON THE THIRD DAY, TIJI ENDS WITH THE CEREMONIAL DESTRUCTION of the evil remains, represented by some long black yak hair and red *torma* cakes minced to a dark red gurry. The remains are chanted over by a lama, as his assistants burn juniper and frankincense, and two lines of monks strike hand drums while those against the wall blow horns. Eventually a procession forms, led by three victory banners, red and white, then the bearers of five braziers bearing the demon's remains, then the horn blowers and monks, then lamas, then court musicians, then the raja and the crown prince and their attendants. The procession pauses for chanting and ceremony at the chortens outside of the main gate, then repeats the ceremonials at the grain-threshing platforms east of the walls, arriving finally at the edge of the town fields.

It is near twilight, a wild mountain light, and on the wind, just beginning to diminish as the cold night falls, white clouds filled with western sun drift past the snow peaks, as snow pigeons wheel over the new green of the spring fields. In the cold light, on the sere sky, Kechar Dzong and its ruined terraces are as pale as Egypt.

The demon's red remnants are set out on an old tiger skin, whereupon they are attacked by bow and arrow, slings, and the old guns. One by one, the braziers filled with the poor devil's remains are overturned upon the ground, each time to a wild cannonade from the old muzzle-loaders and a wave of cheers and smoke. Finally the emptied braziers are removed and the sad remains flailed with the tiger skin to satisfy the crowd that nothing has been overlooked in dispelling the forces of evil from Lo Monthang.

Tiji is over, and tomorrow the people will go home to their own villages. I circumambulate the town for the last time, in cold clear light. [➡ 178]

People flock into Chyodi Monastery for the blessing of Tashi Tenzing during a ritual, as the monks chant and play cymbals.

a mandala of masked dancers dance at Tiji

a sand mandala being constructed for a ritual in Lo Monthang

Lama Pasang, deep in the meditation to embody the deity Dorje Jono, aims his ritual dagger, a purba, *to strike the evil forces that have been bound in the offering cake.*

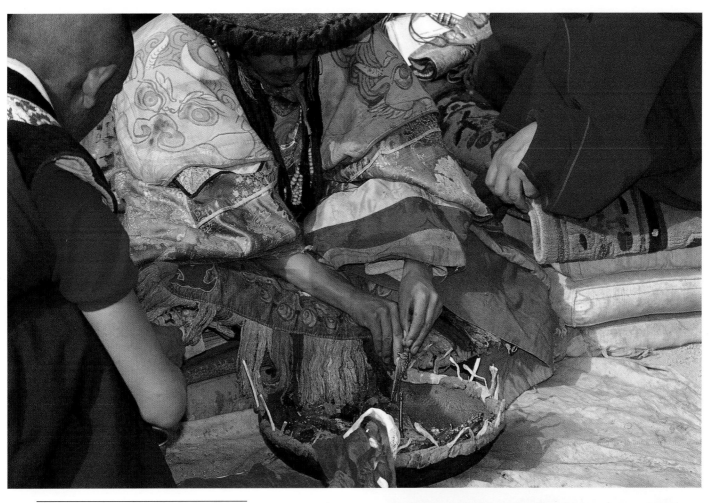

Lama Pasang buries his purba *in the offering.*

The cake is both a symbol of evil being destroyed and an offering to the evil forces.

dancers and audience during the Tiji Ceremony

The devout and the profane, monastic silks and lay brocades — all are part of festivals in Mustang.

masked dancers at the conclusion of Tiji

The raja and Pema Ngotu fire off a matchlock to drive away any lurking evil at the conclusion of Tiji.

This image of "The Coming Buddha," Maitreya (Sanskrit) or Champa (Tibetan), is nearly fifty feet tall, making it one of the largest clay statues in Nepal. Paintings of the subsidiary images behind it are original; the gilding and painting on the body of Champa was done during the last fifteen years. This is the image that the temple is commonly named after.

"May one be liberated as soon as he sees this temple of the body, speech and mind of the Buddhas.

May one be liberated as soon as he hears about it or touches it.

May one be liberated as soon as he prostrates and circumambulates it.

May one be liberated as soon as this temple is even thought of."

—INSCRIPTION IN CHAMPA LHA-KHANG ("TEMPLE OF THE COMING BUDDHA"),
LO MONTHANG, CIRCA 1435

The walls surrounding the image of Champa are over twenty feet high and were originally painted with forty mandalas. The mandalas are tiered in two layers and are about five feet in diameter. Only about twenty-five of these paintings have survived the passage of the past five hundred years. Construction of this temple began ca. A.D. 1415; painting began ca. A.D. 1424; the Champa statue was consecrated (and the temple presumably completed) in A.D. 1435 by the great Tibetan teacher, Ngorchen Kunga Dzangpo.

"Through the diamond-like wisdom of happiness, even the largest mountains are seen in their true reality. I prostrate to the deity, Dorje Sempa, surrounded by eight completely vanquished wrathful ones."

—INSCRIPTION UNDERNEATH THE DORJE SEMPA/NAGA MANDALA

Mandala of the deity Dorje Sempa, surrounded by eight Nagas with their Nagini consorts: the Nagas are pre-Buddhist deities common in Nepal and India; they are shown here vanquished by Dorje Sempa. Nagas are "Lords of The Earth" and thus control rainfall, field fertility and so on. Dorje Sempa is able to command their assistance for followers of Buddhism. The forty mandalas of Champa Lha-khang illustrate a Buddhist text called "The Yoga Tantra."

Vajrasattva is depicted here, underneath the mandala of one thousand Buddhas in Champa Lha-khang, in clear Newar style. Underneath this painting are inscriptions that identify the master painter of Champa Lha-khang as a Newar from Kathmandu Valley. He probably worked with a team of Loba and Tibetan painters for a decade to produce the paintings that embellish this temple.

OPPOSITE ~ *This image of Mahakala, a wrathful protector deity, guards the entrance to Champa Lha-khang, next to the Dorje Sempa/Naga Mandala. The style of this painting, including the crown and the treatment of the fire in background, is clearly of Kathmandu-Newar origin.*

"Whoever sees the body or hears the speech of the deity of this mandala is protected from the shortcomings of the human condition . . ."

—PART OF THE INSCRIPTION UNDERNEATH THE MANDALA OF
ONE THOUSAND BUDDHAS IN CHAMPA LHA-KHANG

ABOVE ~ *A monk carries a stick with a brocade hanging behind. The brocade pattern of Chinese origins is said to be of the Tang period. The painter of this mural probably saw a Tang period brocade, on which he based this painting. The artists of Mustang were exposed to influences from farther afield because of the trade route up and down the Kali Gandaki.*

LEFT ~ *Again this detail of a wall painting in the Tugchen Lha-kang displays clear Chinese influence in the treatment of the robes of this "throne upholder."*

OPPOSITE PAGE ~ *In Tugchen's great hall, the pillars are thirty feet high and all the walls of this one hundred and fifteen-by-sixty five-foot hall were once covered in fine Buddhist murals, such as those visible on the wall behind the monk.*

❖ A WEDDING ❖

The bride Karchung is comforted by her friend Lhamo.
Pemba, a friend of the groom, sips chang *as he waits to*
take Karchung back to the groom's house in Charang.

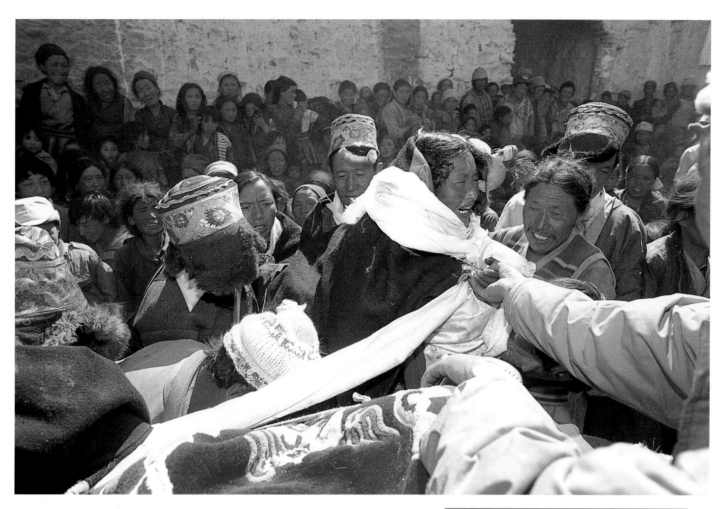

At the climatic moment of Karchung's departure from Lo Monthang, the entire town gathers to see her lifted onto her horse.

Still wailing her protestations at being married off to two brothers she has never met, Karchung is calmed on the outskirts of Lo Monthang; her worried friend, Lhamo, approaches.

Father of the bride, Aungyi, leads the wedding party through the windy pass above Lo Monthang; Karchung, mounted on a horse being led by a member of the groom's party, follows behind.

FOLLOWING PAGES ~ *The mother of the bride shares a joke with a friend.*

⊠ Epilogue

In early June we left Lo Monthang and climbed up to the southern pass and down the farther side, descending across the desert landscapes with their larks and snow finches and rose finches and desert wheatears, a bird I first saw years ago on its winter range in Africa. In midmorning, in that mysterious lull between the north and south winds, the sweet small song of the wheatear (from olde Englishe "white-arse") carries far across the ringing silence.

The old trade route descends the Sumda Khola into the Charang Khola, climbing the far side to the village. At 11,700 feet, Charang is a well-watered and far greener place than Lo, with gardens and neat whitewashed houses and thriving apple trees. (These trees were brought here by Pasang, the Sherpa attendant of Dr. David Snellgrove, whose *Himalayan Pilgrimage*[1] became a useful guide on my trek to Dolpo in 1973; Dr. Snellgrove entered the kingdom of Lo but was allowed no further than Charang.)

Charang Dzong is a five-story fort-palace on the brink of a ravine several hundred feet deep. Climbing narrow steps in the near dark, we find twenty monks in the main chapel, chanting to drums and cymbals from the beautiful twenty-four-karat-gold script on long indigo blue-black pages of the Kanjur — the Tibetan scriptures in one hundred and eight volumes. The *dzong* is the largest left in Lo, and the most massive structure outside Lo Monthang, and in the gompa — like the *dzong,* a mere remnant of its former size — there are many superb *tanka*s (although the two most valuable are not on view, due to last year's theft of sixteen fine *tankas* from Gelling Gompa). More interesting still are the huge caldrons in the kitchen, which suggest that this all but abandoned place with its cold dust and drafty silences once fed and sheltered many hundred monks and lamas.

As the track continues south, the empty mesa crossed two weeks earlier on the way from Tey Khola to Yara and Ghara can be seen faraway to eastward over the broad river, and also the strange black pinnacles first observed from the high mountain trail to Tey. Above Gemi Khola, at an extraordinary high wall of carved prayer stones well over a hundred yards in length, are the only travellers we have come across north of Kagbeni, a band of scurvy drovers whose large goat herd is burdened with small sacks of barley.

---

[1] *Himalayan Pilgrimage,* David Snellgrove. Boston: Shambhala, 1981.

The fields of pink are buckwheat; those of yellow, wheat; those of green, barley. On the crown of the ridge above are the ruins of the fort of Gelling; below a chorten; the red buildings are temples.

Gemi, where a man shows us scars of a wolf bite on his *dzo,* is still lower and more well-watered than Charang, with many trees, a spare palace of the raja, and three cave villages in the cliffs upriver. Here, next morning, Laird and I part company. He is returning to Lo Monthang, then on into the nomad country on his quest for *mehti,* taking Ongdi with him. ("All I do is carry," Ongdi says. "When they tell me to come, I come, and where they tell me to go, I go. The rest of the time I just sit in the corner, and I listen carefully.") I envy Tom that journey but am content with this one, and happy that he rang me up from Kathmandu. He has been a superb guide and an intelligent companion, and I am grateful to him.

Ordinarily the journey from Gemi to Jomsom takes three days. Since Gelling Gompa has been locked up due to the thefts, we did not bother to descend the plateau into Gelling but rode on past through the high country under the western peaks where humans were absent and junipers and caragana common.

Over the last high pass, where we dismounted, flew a golden eagle.

Lying back against a rock on a rare day without strong wind, I contemplated the high face of Nilgiri. This northwest peak of the Annapurnas rose into the southern sky like a white colossus, whiter even than the soft white clouds far out beyond the deep purple crescent of the Kali Gandaki Gorge, beyond the mountains, as warm and peaceful as the monsoon clouds over the Indian Ocean.

As the trail descends, the green increases in the valleys, and birches appear in the ravines and lower hillsides. Because June has come, and because these villages under high ridges receive more rain, the field crops and wild flowers are more profuse than they were in May. At Samar, where we had planned to spend the night, we decide to take advantage of good weather, and by late afternoon are descending the awesome Gyakhar canyon, arriving near sunset at Chaili. Peering down from the rim, I can see the dark and narrow portal where long ago, or so it seems, we entered the Kali Gandaki's upper gorge. Tomorrow we shall descend to the main river and make our way south again to Jomsom, in the shadow of the Himalaya.

Sunset still gilds the desert hills above the temple of Ghara as the full moon rises; prayer flag and child.

Chyodi Monastery, surrounded by the houses of the monks,
within the walls of Lo Monthang: summer and winter

FOLLOWING PAGES ~ *Just south of the Nepal/Tibet border looking south across the*
16,000-foot watershed plateau between the Ganges and the Bhramaputra-Tsangpo.
To the south, beyond all of Mustang, which lies hidden beneath this plateau, the deep
gorge of the Kali Gandaki is visible as a notch (between Annapurna and Dhaulagiri)
in the long north face of the Himalayan Mountains.

PETER MATTHIESSEN was born in New York City and had already begun his writing career by the time he graduated from Yale University in 1950. The following year, he founded the *Paris Review*. Mr. Matthiessen's career as a naturalist and explorer has resulted in numerous outstanding works of nonfiction, among them *The Tree Where Man Was Born*, which was nominated for a National Book Award, and *The Snow Leopard*, which won it. His other works of nonfiction include *The Cloud Forest* and *Under the Mountain Wall* (which together received an Award of Merit from the National Institute of Arts and Letters), *Nine-Headed Dragon River*, *The Wind Birds*, *Blue Meridian*, *Sal Si Puedes*, *Sand Rivers*, *In the Spirit of Crazy Horse*, *Indian Country*, *Men's Lives*, and *African Silences*. He has published six novels, including *At Play in the Fields of the Lord*, which was nominated for a National Book Award, *Killing Mister Watson*, and *Far Tortuga*, as well as the collection *On the River Styx and Other Stories*.

Peter Matthiessen

THOMAS LAIRD is an American photographer, writer, and ethnographer, who has lived in Nepal for more than 20 years. He was the only foreign photographer to cover all major events of the Nepali "People's Movement" of 1990. His photographs have appeared in *National Geographic*, *GEO*, *Stern*, *Le Figaro*, *Conde Nast Traveler* and many other publications around the world, and he is the Nepal correspondent for *Asiaweek*. His explorations in Asia have taken him on more than 50 treks throughout the Himalayas. He was the first Westerner to enter Mustang when it was opened in 1991.

Thomas Laird

Left to right: Assistant police inspector G. B. Kafle (government liaison officer), Karma Sherpa (cook and logistics master), Tashi (horses), Geljen Sherpa (cook and camera assistant), Ongdi (master of the bags, and all chang *ever brewed).*

One of the first tourists to arrive in Mustang hands out Polaroids to the delight of the Loba.

Namgyal, Trenkar and ruins in winter

❖ ACKNOWLEDGMENTS

IT WOULD NOT HAVE BEEN POSSIBLE FOR PETER MATTHIESSEN OR MYSELF TO work in Mustang without the understanding, permission and support of His Majesty's Government of Nepal. In particular I would like to thank the individuals, in office in 1991, who pushed this project forward from its inception: Minister of Tourism Ram Hari Joshy, Home Minister Sher Bahadur Deuba, Prime Minister G.P. Koirala, and their staff. Sincere thanks are also extended to civil servants in the Ministry of Communication, the Department of Information, the Home Ministry, the Department of Tourism, the Department of Immigration, and the office of the Inspector General of Police.

A hearty thank you is also due to so many in Mustang. The Loba — with the encouragement of Raja Jigme Palbar Bista — accepted me into their homes, temples and lives for nearly one year. Without the unfailing hospitality they provided, the photographs in this book would not exist. The following merit special thanks: the raja, rani and crown prince of Lo, Khenpo Tashi Tenzing and the Monks of Chyodi Monastery, Amji Tashi Chusang, Sona Tsangmo, Amji Gyatso, Pema Ongdi, Karchung and their son Gyatso, Chyodi Aungyel, Dhoka, Uten, Tamde Wangyal, Yamzong Bista, Pema Tutu Bista, Jamyang and Ri-Dorje, Kunga Palden and his son Pasang Lama, Temba Gylatsen Bista and his sons Indra and Rajendra, Pema Ngotu, Lakpa Tsering, Aungyi Pama Lama, Jabyang Lama, Karma Wangyel, Bishnu Duki, Lobsang Bista, his wife Tsela and their children, Tsewang Zintin and Maya, Jabyang Chusang Bista, Raju Bista, Chuda Gurung, Tashi Aungyi, Tsedup, Chudzong Lama, Luri Lama and Risangmo's son Ongdi.

Friends and family who contributed immensely to this project include Francesco Papalia, Keith Dowman, Roberto Vitali, Ian Alsop, David Hurst, Peter Blessing, Kelly Kammerer, Meen Vajracharya, Muktan, Col. Lama, Shanti Maharjan, John Schneeberger, Bruce McElfresh, Julia Chang Bloch, Tracy Parker, Micheal Silpa, Jerri Marriot, Manojani Pradhan, Dana Nelson, Kathleen Klech, Tom Wallace, George and Annie, James Pryor, Charles Gay, Vittorrio Chiaudano, Judy Chase, Hugh Swift, Toni Neubauer, Bill Abbott, Robert and Mahalia, Lee and Danny, Ian Baker, Thomas Kelly, Carol Dunham, Eric Valli, Diane Summers, Nick Seely, Nick and Chrissy Gregory, E. Lobue, Jimmy Roberts, Sonam Gyalpo, Robin Marston, Jeff Greenwald, Hugh Moss, Krishna Basnet, Barend Toet, Kate Russell, TCS, Bonnie and Earl Fenner, and Lois and Tommy Laird.

Many thanks to Nikon for 35mm cameras, lenses and flash units; Pentax for the 6x7; Widelux for the panorama camera; Chimera for soft boxes; Marmot for clothes; Vasque for boots; and Fuji for film. Special thanks to Samuel Bercholz and Magnus Bartlett, for believing in this book.

I could never have taken off to Mustang for a year without the support of my wife, Jann Fenner, and her daemons Chulu, Tashi and Garphu.

For all of you I hope this book is some repayment for what you have invested in it.

—Thomas Laird